NINJA FOODI 800

BY LEO LIONELL

Breakfast Muffins with Egg Cups

Prep Time: 5-10 min.
Cooking Time: 14 min.
Number of Servings: 4-6

Ingredients:
2 tablespoons butter, melted
12 ounces broccoli florets
8 medium eggs
2 tablespoons milk
Ground black pepper and salt, to taste
¼ cup of water
¾ cup cheddar cheese, shredded

Directions:
1. Take Foodi multi-cooker, arrange it over a cooking platform, and open the top lid.
2. In the pot, add the butter; Select "SEAR/SAUTÉ" mode and select "MD: HI" pressure level.
3. Press "STOP/START." After about 4-5 minutes, the butter will start simmering.
4. Add the broccoli and cook (while stirring) until it becomes softened for 2-3 minutes.
5. Add in water, pepper, and salt; stir the mixture.
6. Seal the multi-cooker by locking it with the pressure lid; ensure to keep the pressure release valve locked/sealed.
7. Select "PRESSURE" mode and select the "HI" pressure level. Then, set timer to 7 minutes and press "STOP/START"; it will start the cooking process by building up inside pressure.
8. When the timer goes off, quick release pressure by adjusting the pressure valve to the VENT. After pressure gets released, open the pressure lid.
9. Select "SEAR/SAUTÉ" mode and select the "MD" pressure level; add the milk and eggs, and combine. Stir-cook for 2-3 minutes.
10. Add the cheese and stir well.
11. Seal the multi-cooker by locking it with the crisping lid; ensure to keep the pressure release valve locked/sealed.
12. Select the "AIR CRISP" mode and adjust the 320°F temperature level. Then, set timer to 2 minutes and press "STOP/START"; it will start the cooking process by building up inside pressure.

13. When the timer goes off, quick release pressure by adjusting the pressure valve to the VENT.
14. After pressure gets released, open the pressure lid.
15. Serve warm and enjoy!

Nutritional Values (Per Serving):
Calories: 214
Fat: 15g
Saturated Fat: 5.5g
Trans Fat: 0g
Carbohydrates: 18g
Fiber: 1.5g
Sodium: 248mg
Protein: 13.5g

Breakfast Egg Ramekins

Prep Time: 5 min.
Cooking Time: 3 min.
Number of Servings: 4

Ingredients:
4 large eggs
4 small slices feta cheese
1 cup water
2 large ripe tomatoes, halved
2 tablespoon Parmesan cheese, grated
1 teaspoon herbs of your choice, chopped
Cooking spray as required
Black pepper and salt to taste

Directions:
1. Take four ramekins and grease with some cooking spray. Crack one egg in each ramekin and season to taste with some black pepper and salt.
2. Cover the ramekins with aluminum foil.
3. In the pot, add water and place a trivet or rack inside the pot. Place the ramekins over the trivet or rack.
4. Seal the multi-cooker by locking it with the pressure lid; ensure to keep the pressure release valve locked/sealed.
5. Select the "STEAM" mode and select the "HI" pressure level. Then, set timer to 3 minutes and press "STOP/START"; it will start the cooking process by building up inside pressure.
6. When the timer goes off, quick release pressure by adjusting the pressure valve to the VENT. After pressure gets released, open the pressure lid.
7. Divide the tomatoes, feta cheese in serving plates; flip the ramekins, and add them to serving plates.
8. Season with black pepper and salt; serve with the Parmesan and herbs on top.

Nutritional Values (Per Serving):
Calories: 346
Fat: 29g
Saturated Fat: 3.5g
Trans Fat: 0g
Carbohydrates: 14.5g
Fiber: 2g
Sodium: 528mg
Protein: 19g

Classic Egg Bacon Breakfast

Prep Time: 5-10 min.
Cooking Time: 8 min.
Number of Servings: 2

Ingredients:
1 tablespoon chopped parsley
2 medium eggs, whisked
2 cooked bacon strips, chopped
Black pepper and salt to the taste

Directions:
1. In a mixing bowl, beat the eggs. One by one, add other ingredients and combine well.
2. Take a baking pan or cake pan; grease it with some cooking spray, vegetable oil, or butter.
3. Add the egg mixture and wrap the pan with aluminum foil.
4. Take Ninja Foodi multi-cooker, arrange it over a cooking platform, and open the top lid.
5. In the pot, add water and place a reversible rack inside the pot. Place the pan over the rack.
6. Seal the multi-cooker by locking it with the crisping lid; ensure to keep the pressure release valve locked/sealed.
7. Select "BAKE/ROAST" mode and adjust the 400°F temperature level. Then, set timer to 8 minutes and press "STOP/START"; it will start the cooking process by building up inside pressure.
8. When the timer goes off, quick release pressure by adjusting the pressure valve to the VENT. After pressure gets released, open the pressure lid.
9. Serve warm and enjoy!

Nutritional Values (Per Serving):
Calories: 135
Fat: 10g
Saturated Fat: 4.5g
Trans Fat: 0g
Carbohydrates: 1g
Fiber: 0g
Sodium: 458mg
Protein: 9g

Healthy Apple Oats

Prep Time: 5-10 min.
Cooking Time: 11 min.
Number of Servings: 4

Ingredients:
¼ cup apple cider vinegar
½ teaspoon vanilla extract
1 tablespoon ground cinnamon
½ teaspoon ground nutmeg
2 cups steel-cut oats
2 apples, peeled, cored, and diced
3 ¾ cups water
½ cup dried cranberries
⅛ teaspoon sea salt
Maple syrup to taste

Directions:
1. Take Ninja Foodi multi-cooker, arrange it over a cooking platform, and open the top lid.
2. In the pot, add the oats, water, vinegar, cinnamon, nutmeg, vanilla, cranberries, apples, and salt.
3. Seal the multi-cooker by locking it with the pressure lid; ensure to keep the pressure release valve locked/sealed.
4. Select "PRESSURE" mode and select the "HI" pressure level. Then, set timer to 11 minutes and press "STOP/START"; it will start the cooking process by building up inside pressure.
5. When the timer goes off, naturally release inside pressure for about 8-10 minutes. Then, quick-release pressure by adjusting the pressure valve to the VENT.
6. After pressure gets released, open the pressure lid.
7. Serve warm with the maple syrup and some berries on top.

Nutritional Values (Per Serving):
Calories: 374
Fat: 6.5g
Saturated Fat: 1g
Trans Fat: 0g
Carbohydrates: 52.5g
Fiber: 9g
Sodium: 103mg
Protein: 14g

Healthy Berry Oatmeal

Prep Time: 5-10 min.
Cooking Time: 10 min.
Number of Servings: 4

Ingredients:
2 raspberries, sliced
½ cup dried cranberries
¼ cup plain vinegar
2 cups oatmeal
3 ¾ cups water
1 tablespoon cinnamon powder
½ teaspoon nutmeg powder
½ teaspoon vanilla extract
⅛ teaspoon salt
Honey to drizzle

Directions:

1. Take Ninja Foodi multi-cooker, arrange it over a cooking platform, and open the top lid.
2. In the pot, add the oatmeal, nutmeg, cinnamon, water, vinegar, vanilla, cranberries, raspberries, and salt; stir the mixture.
3. Seal the multi-cooker by locking it with the pressure lid; ensure to keep the pressure release valve locked/sealed.
4. Select "PRESSURE" mode and select the "HI" pressure level. Then, set timer to 10 minutes and press "STOP/START"; it will start the cooking process by building up inside pressure.
5. When the timer goes off, naturally release inside pressure for about 8-10 minutes. Then, quick release pressure by adjusting the pressure valve to VENT.
6. After pressure gets released, open the pressure lid.
7. Serve warm topped with some more cranberries and honey; enjoy!

Nutritional Values (Per Serving):
Calories: 304
Fat: 5g
Saturated Fat: 1g
Trans Fat: 0g
Carbohydrates: 37.5g
Fiber: 12g
Sodium: 419mg
Protein: 6g

Bacon with Hash & Eggs

Prep Time: 5-10 min.
Cooking Time: 40 min.
Number of Servings: 4

Ingredients:
2 russet potatoes, peeled and diced
6 slices bacon, chopped
1 yellow onion, diced
4 eggs
1 teaspoon freshly ground black pepper
1 teaspoon garlic salt
1 teaspoon paprika
1 teaspoon sea salt

Directions:
1. Take Ninja Foodi multi-cooker, arrange it over a cooking platform, and open the top lid.
2. In the pot, add the oil; Select "SEAR/SAUTÉ" mode and select "MD: HI" pressure level.
3. Press "STOP/START." After about 4-5 minutes, the oil will start simmering.
4. Add the bacon and cook (while stirring) for about 5 minutes until it becomes crispy.
5. Add the potatoes and onions; season with the paprika, sea salt, pepper, and garlic salt.
6. Seal the multi-cooker by locking it with the crisping lid; ensure to keep the pressure release valve locked/sealed.
7. Select "BAKE/ROAST" mode and adjust the 350°F temperature level. Then, set timer to 25 minutes and press "STOP/START"; it will start the cooking process by building up inside pressure.
8. When the timer goes off, quick release pressure by adjusting the pressure valve to the VENT.
9. Open the lid, crack the eggs over the cooked mixture.
10. Seal the multi-cooker by locking it with the crisping lid; ensure to keep the pressure release valve locked/sealed.
11. Select "BAKE/ROAST" mode and adjust the 350°F temperature level. Then, set timer to 10 minutes and press "STOP/START"; it will start the cooking process by building up inside pressure.
12. When the timer goes off, quick release pressure by adjusting the pressure valve to VENT. After pressure gets released, open the pressure lid.
13. Serve warm and enjoy!

Nutritional Values (Per Serving):

Calories: 329
Fat: 23g
Saturated Fat: 8g
Trans Fat: 0g
Carbohydrates: 23.5g
Fiber: 3g
Sodium: 983mg
Protein: 14g

Classic Cinnamon Almond Oats

Prep Time: 5-10 min.
Cooking Time: 15 min.
Number of Servings: 4

Ingredients:
½ cup slivered almonds, blanched
2 tablespoons butter, unsalted
1 cup steel-cut oats
½ teaspoon vanilla extract
¼ teaspoon ground cinnamon
¼ teaspoon kosher salt
2 tablespoons sugar
2 cups water
1 cup whole milk

Directions:
1. Take Ninja Foodi multi-cooker, arrange it over a cooking platform, and open the top lid.
2. In the pot, arrange a reversible rack and place the Crisping Basket over the rack. In the basket, add the almonds.
3. Seal the multi-cooker by locking it with the crisping lid; ensure to keep the pressure release valve locked/sealed.
4. Select the "AIR CRISP" mode and adjust the 375°F temperature level. Then, set timer to 5 minutes and press "STOP/START"; it will start the cooking process by building up inside pressure.
5. When the timer goes off, quick release pressure by adjusting the pressure valve to the VENT.
6. After pressure gets released, open the pressure lid. Set aside the almonds and take out the basket and rack.
7. In the pot, add the butter; Select "SEAR/SAUTÉ" mode and select "MD: HI" pressure level.
8. Press "STOP/START." After about 4-5 minutes, the butter will start simmering.
9. Add the oats and cook (while stirring) for about 2-3 minutes until they become softened. Mix in the Add the salt, sugar, vanilla, cinnamon, water, and milk.
10. Seal the multi-cooker by locking it with the pressure lid; ensure to keep the pressure release valve locked/sealed.
11. Select "PRESSURE" mode and select the "HI" pressure level. Then, set timer to 10 minutes and press "STOP/START"; it will start the cooking process by building up inside pressure.
12. When the timer goes off, naturally release inside pressure for about 8-10 minutes. Then, quick release pressure by adjusting the pressure valve to the VENT.
13. After pressure gets released, open the pressure lid.
14. Serve warm with toasted almonds on top and enjoy!

Nutritional Values (Per Serving):

Calories: 365
Fat: 19.5g
Saturated Fat: 6g
Trans Fat: 0g
Carbohydrates: 39g
Fiber: 7g
Sodium: 142mg
Protein: 2g

Egg Broccoli Quiche

Prep Time: 10 min.
Cooking Time: 20 min.
Number of Servings: 6

Ingredients:
8 medium eggs
½ cup milk
1 cup Cheddar cheese, shredded
1 tablespoon extra-virgin olive oil
1 teaspoon sea salt
1 teaspoon ground black pepper
2 garlic cloves, minced
1 yellow onion, chopped
2 cups broccoli florets, thinly sliced
1 piecrust, at room temperature

Directions:
1. In a mixing bowl, whisk the eggs; add the milk, salt, and pepper. Add the Cheddar cheese and whisk well.
2. Take Ninja Foodi multi-cooker, arrange it over a cooking platform, and open the top lid.
3. In the pot, add the oil; Select the "SEAR/SAUTÉ" mode and select the "HI" pressure level.
4. Press "STOP/START." After about 4-5 minutes, the oil will start simmering.
5. Add the onions, garlic, and cook (while stirring) for 4-5 minutes until they become softened and translucent.
6. Add the broccoli; sauté for another 5 minutes.
7. Add the egg mixture over and gently stir-cook for 1 minute until the eggs cook well and incorporate.
8. In the pie crust, add the mixture. And fold the edges. For heat escape, make a small cut in the center of the piecrust.
9. Seal the multi-cooker by locking it with the crisping lid; ensure to keep the pressure release valve locked/sealed.
10. Select "BROIL" mode and select the "HI" pressure level. Then, set timer to 10 minutes and press "STOP/START"; it will start the cooking process by building up inside pressure.
11. When the timer goes off, quick release pressure by adjusting the pressure valve to the VENT.
12. After pressure gets released, open the pressure lid.
13. Slice and serve the pie warm and enjoy!

Nutritional Values (Per Serving):

Calories: 369
Fat: 25.5g
Saturated Fat: 9g
Trans Fat: 0g
Carbohydrates: 26g
Fiber: 3g
Sodium: 753mg
Protein: 16g

Kale Sausage Breakfast

Prep Time: 5-10 min.
Cooking Time: 10 min.
Number of Servings: 4
Ingredients:

1 medium sweet yellow onion
4 medium eggs
4 sausage links
2 cups kale, chopped
1 cup mushrooms
Olive oil as required

Directions:

1. Take Ninja Foodi Grill, arrange it over your kitchen platform, and open the top lid.
2. Arrange the grill grate and close the top lid.
3. Press "GRILL" and select the "HIGH" grill function. Adjust the timer to 5 minutes and then press "START/STOP." Ninja Foodi will start pre-heating.
4. Ninja Foodi is preheated and ready to cook when it starts to beep. After you hear a beep, open the top lid.
5. Arrange the sausages over the grill grate.
6. Close the top lid and cook for 2 minutes. Now open the top lid, flip the sausages.
7. Close the top lid and cook for three more minutes.
8. Take out the grilled sausages.
9. Take a multi-purpose pan and lightly grease it with some cooking oil. Spread the onion, mushrooms, and kale; add the grilled sausages and crack the eggs in between the sausages.
10. Open the lid and arrange the pan directly inside the pot.
11. Press "BAKE" and adjust the temperature to 350°F. Adjust the timer to 5 minutes and then press "START/STOP."
12. Close the top lid and allow it to cook until the timer reads zero.
13. Serve warm.
14.

Nutritional Values (Per Serving):

Calories: 236
Fat: 12g
Saturated Fat: 2g
Trans Fat: 0g
Carbohydrates: 17g
Fiber: 4g
Sodium: 369mg
Protein: 18g

Coconut Breakfast Bagels

Prep Time: 5-10 min.
Cooking Time: 8 min.
Number of Servings: 4
Ingredients:
1 cup fine sugar
2 tablespoons black coffee, prepared and cooled down
4 bagels, halved
1/4 cup coconut milk
2 tablespoons coconut flakes
Directions:
1. Take Ninja Foodi Grill, arrange it over your kitchen platform, and open the top lid.
2. Arrange the grill grate and close the top lid.
3. Press "GRILL" and select the "MED" grill function. Adjust the timer to 4 minutes and then press "START/STOP." Ninja Foodi will start pre-heating.
4. Ninja Foodi is preheated and ready to cook when it starts to beep. After you hear a beep, open the top lid.
5. Arrange 2 bagels over the grill grate.
6. Close the top lid and cook for 2 minutes. Now open the top lid, flip the bagels.
7. Close the top lid and cook for 2 more minutes.
8. Allow cooking until the timer reads zero. Divide into serving plates.
9. Grill the remaining bagels in a similar way. In a mixing bowl, whisk the remaining ingredients.
10. Serve the grilled bagels with the prepared sauce on top.

Nutritional Values (Per Serving):

Calories: 395
Fat: 23g
Saturated Fat: 12g
Trans Fat: 0g
Carbohydrates: 42.5g
Fiber: 4g
Sodium: 358mg
Protein: 18.5g

Pineapple French Toast

Prep Time: 5-10 min.
Cooking Time: 15 min.
Number of Servings: 4-5
Ingredients:
10 bread slices
1/4 cup sugar
1/4 cup milk
3 large eggs
1 cup coconut milk
10 slices pineapple (1/4-inch-thick), peeled
1/2 cup coconut flakes
Cooking spray
Directions:
1. In a mixing bowl, whisk the coconut milk, sugar, eggs, and milk. Dip the bread in this mixture and set aside for about 2 minutes.
2. Take Ninja Foodi Grill, arrange it over your kitchen platform, and open the top lid.
3. Arrange the grill grate and close the top lid.
4. Press "GRILL" and select the "MED" grill function. Adjust the timer to 4 minutes and then press "START/STOP." Ninja Foodi will start pre-heating.
5. Ninja Foodi is preheated and ready to cook when it starts to beep. After you hear a beep, open the top lid.
6. Arrange half the bread slices over the grill grate.
7. Close the top lid and cook for 2 minutes. Now open the top lid, flip the slices.
8. Close the top lid and cook for 2 more minutes.
9. Allow cooking until the timer reads zero. Divide into serving plates.
10. Repeat with the remaining slices. And then grill the pineapple slices with the same amount of time (flipping after 2 minutes).
11. Serve warm with the grilled bread topped with some coconut flakes.

Nutritional Values (Per Serving):

Calories: 202
Fat: 15g
Saturated Fat: 4g
Trans Fat: 0g
Carbohydrates: 49g
Fiber: 3g
Sodium: 214mg
Protein: 8g

Creamed French Toast

Prep Time: 5-10 min.
Cooking Time: 4 min.
Number of Servings: 2-3
Ingredients:
Juice of ½ orange
3 slices challah bread
2 medium eggs
½ quart strawberries, quartered
1 tablespoon balsamic vinegar
1/4 cup heavy cream
1 tablespoon honey
1 teaspoon orange zest
½ teaspoon vanilla extract
1/2 sprig rosemary
Salt to taste
Directions:
1. Take a foil sheet and add the strawberries, balsamic vinegar, orange juice, rosemary, and zest. Fold edges to create a pocket.
2. In a mixing bowl, whisk the egg; add the cream, honey, vanilla, and a pinch of salt and whisk again.
3. Dip the bread slices to coat evenly in the mixture.
4. Take Ninja Foodi Grill, arrange it over your kitchen platform, and open the top lid.
5. Arrange the grill grate and close the top lid.
6. Press "GRILL" and select the "MED" grill function. Adjust the timer to 4 minutes and then press "START/STOP." Ninja Foodi will start pre-heating.
7. Ninja Foodi is preheated and ready to cook when it starts to beep. After you hear a beep, open the top lid.
8. Arrange the foil packet and bread slices over the grill grate.
9. Close the top lid and cook for 2 minutes. Now open the top lid, flip the flip.
10. Close the top lid and cook for 2 more minutes.
11. Allow cooking until the timer reads zero. Divide into serving plates.
12. Serve warm the bread with the strawberry mixture.

Nutritional Values (Per Serving):
Calories: 369
Fat: 11.5g
Saturated Fat: 5g
Trans Fat: 0g
Carbohydrates: 36g
Fiber: 3.5g
Sodium: 186mg
Protein: 15g

Chicken Hot Potato

Prep Time: 5-10 min.
Cooking Time: 25 min.
Number of Servings: 4
Ingredients:

2 teaspoons Worcestershire sauce
¼ cup chicken stock
1 tablespoon olive oil
1 ½ pounds medium Yukon Gold potatoes, quartered
4 chicken thighs, with bone and skin
½ teaspoon kosher salt
2 tablespoons melted butter
2 teaspoons curry powder
1 teaspoon dried oregano leaves
½ teaspoon dry mustard
½ teaspoon garlic, minced
¼ teaspoon paprika
2 dashes hot pepper sauce of your choice

Directions:
1. Sprinkle the chicken evenly with the salt.
2. In a mixing bowl, add the butter, Worcestershire sauce, curry powder, oregano, dry mustard, granulated garlic, paprika, and hot pepper sauce. Whisk to combine well.
3. Add the chicken stock and combine.
4. Take Ninja Foodi multi-cooker, arrange it over a cooking platform, and open the top lid.
5. In the pot, add the oil; Select "SEAR/SAUTÉ" mode and select "MD: HI" pressure level.
6. Press "STOP/START." After about 4-5 minutes, the oil will start simmering.
7. Add the chicken thighs with skin side touching the pot and stir-cook for about 5 minutes to brown evenly. Remove from the pot.
8. In the pot, add the potatoes and stir; add half the sauce and combine. Arrange the chicken thighs on top and top with the remaining sauce.
9. Seal the multi-cooker by locking it with the pressure lid; ensure to keep the pressure release valve locked/sealed.
10. Select "PRESSURE" mode and select the "HI" pressure level. Then, set timer to 3 minutes and press "STOP/START"; it will start the cooking process by building up inside pressure.

11. When the timer goes off, quick release pressure by adjusting the pressure valve to the VENT. After pressure gets released, open the pressure lid.
12. Take out the chicken and arrange them over the reversible rack. Spoon some cooked sauce over it. Keep the potato mixture in the pot.
13. Seal the multi-cooker by locking it with the crisping lid; ensure to keep the pressure release valve locked/sealed.
14. Select "BAKE/ROAST" mode and adjust the 375°F temperature level. Then, set timer to 15 minutes and press "STOP/START"; it will start the cooking process by building up inside pressure.
15. When the timer goes off, quick release pressure by adjusting the pressure valve to the VENT. After pressure gets released, open the pressure lid.
16. Serve warm and enjoy!

Nutritional Values (Per Serving):
Calories: 539
Fat: 22.5g
Saturated Fat: 7g
Trans Fat: 0g
Carbohydrates: 53.5g
Fiber: 5g
Sodium: 411mg
Protein: 24.5g

Classic Honey Soy Chicken

Prep Time: 5-10 min.
Cooking Time: 18 min.
Number of Servings: 4

Ingredients:
4 boneless, skinless chicken breast, cut into small pieces
4 garlic cloves, smashed
1 onion, diced
½ cup honey
2 tablespoon lime juice
2 teaspoon sesame oil
3 tablespoon soy sauce
1 tablespoon water
1 tablespoon cornstarch
1 teaspoon rice vinegar
Black pepper and salt to taste

Directions:
1. In a mixing bowl, add the honey, sesame oil, lime juice, soy sauce, and rice vinegar. Combine well.
2. Take Ninja Foodi multi-cooker, arrange it over a cooking platform, and open the top lid.
3. In the pot, add the onion, chicken, and garlic; add the soy sauce mixture and stir gently.
4. Seal the multi-cooker by locking it with the pressure lid; ensure to keep the pressure release valve locked/sealed.
5. Select "PRESSURE" mode and select the "HI" pressure level. Then, set timer to 15 minutes and press "STOP/START"; it will start the cooking process by building up inside pressure.
6. When the timer goes off, quick release pressure by adjusting the pressure valve to the VENT. After pressure gets released, open the pressure lid.
7. In a bowl, mix water and cornstarch until well dissolved.
8. Select "SEAR/SAUTÉ" mode and select the "MD" pressure level; add the cornstarch mixture in the pot and combine it. Stir-cook for 2 minutes.
9. Serve warm.

Nutritional Values (Per Serving):

Calories: 493
Fat: 8.5g
Saturated Fat: 1g
Trans Fat: 0g
Carbohydrates: 44.5g
Fiber: 5g
Sodium: 712mg
Protein: 41.5g

Mexican Chicken Soup

Prep Time: 5-10 min.
Cooking Time: 15 min.
Number of Servings: 6

Ingredients:
1 (14.5 ounces) can black beans, rinsed and drained
14 ounces canned whole tomatoes, chopped
2 cups corn kernels
¼ cup cheddar cheese, shredded
5 chicken thighs, boneless, skinless
5 cups chicken broth
1 tablespoon ground cumin
½ teaspoon dried oregano
2 tablespoon tomato puree
1 tablespoon chili powder
3 cloves garlic, minced
2 stemmed jalapeno peppers, cored and chopped
Fresh cilantro, chopped to garnish

Directions:
1. Take Ninja Foodi multi-cooker, arrange it over a cooking platform, and open the top lid.
2. In the pot, add the chicken, chicken stock, cumin, oregano, garlic, tomato puree, tomatoes, chili powder, and jalapeno peppers; stir the mixture.
3. Seal the multi-cooker by locking it with the pressure lid; ensure to keep the pressure release valve locked/sealed.
4. Select "PRESSURE" mode and select the "HI" pressure level. Then, set timer to 10 minutes and press "STOP/START"; it will start the cooking process by building up inside pressure.
5. When the timer goes off, quick release pressure by adjusting the pressure valve to the VENT. After pressure gets released, open the pressure lid.
6. Shred the chicken and add it back in the pot.
7. Select "SEAR/SAUTÉ" mode and select "MD: HI" pressure level; add the beans and corn and combine. Stir-cook for 4 minutes.
8. Add the cilantro and cheese on top; serve warm.

Nutritional Values (Per Serving):

Calories: 408

Fat: 15g

Saturated Fat: 3g

Trans Fat: 0g

Carbohydrates: 31g

Fiber: 9g

Sodium: 548mg

Protein: 34g

Creamy Chicken Soup

Prep Time: 5-10 min.
Cooking Time: 15 min.
Number of Servings: 5-6

Ingredients:
2 large boneless, skinless chicken breasts, cut into small pieces
1 cup carrots, chopped
1 cup red onion, chopped
4 ounces mascarpone cheese
6 ounces quinoa, rinsed
4 cups chicken broth
1 cup milk
1 cup heavy cream
1 cup celery, chopped
2 tablespoons butter, melted
1 tablespoon parsley, chopped
Black pepper and salt to taste

Directions:
1. Take Ninja Foodi multi-cooker, arrange it over a cooking platform, and open the top lid.
2. In the pot, add the butter; Select "SEAR/SAUTÉ" mode and select "MD: HI" pressure level.
3. Press "STOP/START." After about 4-5 minutes, the butter will start simmering.
4. Add the onions, carrots, celery, and cook (while stirring) until they become softened and translucent.
5. Add the chicken broth, parsley, quinoa, and chicken; combine well — season with black pepper and salt to taste.
6. Seal the multi-cooker by locking it with the pressure lid; ensure to keep the pressure release valve locked/sealed.
7. Select "PRESSURE" mode and select the "HI" pressure level. Then, set timer to 5 minutes and press "STOP/START"; it will start the cooking process by building up inside pressure.
8. When the timer goes off, quick release pressure by adjusting the pressure valve to the VENT. After pressure gets released, open the pressure lid.
9. Select "SEAR/SAUTÉ" mode and select the "MD" pressure level; add the cheese, milk, and cream and combine. Stir-cook for 4 minutes.
10. Serve warm and enjoy!

Nutritional Values (Per Serving):

Calories: 493

Fat: 27.5g

Saturated Fat: 6g

Trans Fat: 0g

Carbohydrates: 30.5g

Fiber: 3g

Sodium: 657mg

Protein: 25g

Turkey Potato Pie

Prep Time: 5-10 min.
Cooking Time: 26 min.
Number of Servings: 5-6

Ingredients:
1 onion, diced
2 garlic cloves, minced
2 pounds boneless turkey breasts, cut into 1-inch cubes
2 Yukon Gold potatoes, diced
1 cup chicken broth
½ stick unsalted butter
½ teaspoon sea salt
½ teaspoon black pepper
2 cups mixed vegetables of your choice
½ cup heavy (whipping) cream
1 refrigerated piecrust

Directions:
1. Take Ninja Foodi multi-cooker, arrange it over a cooking platform, and open the top lid.
2. In the pot, add the butter; Select "SEAR/SAUTÉ" mode and select "MD: HI" pressure level.
3. Press "STOP/START." After about 4-5 minutes, the butter will start simmering.
4. Add the onion, garlic, and cook (while stirring) until it becomes softened and translucent for 2-3 minutes.
5. Add the turkey, potatoes, and broth; stir gently — season with the ground black pepper and salt.
6. Seal the multi-cooker by locking it with the pressure lid; ensure to keep the pressure release valve locked/sealed.
7. Select "PRESSURE" mode and select the "HI" pressure level. Then, set timer to 10 minutes and press "STOP/START"; it will start the cooking process by building up inside pressure.
8. When the timer goes off, quick release pressure by adjusting the pressure valve to the VENT. After pressure gets released, open the pressure lid.
9. Select "SEAR/SAUTÉ" mode and select the "MD" pressure level; add the cream and vegetables and combine. Stir-cook for 3 minutes to thicken the sauce.
10. In the pie crust, add the cooked mixture and fold the edges. Make a few cuts on top for steam escape.
11. Place the pie crust in the pot.

12. Seal the multi-cooker by locking it with the crisping lid; ensure to keep the pressure release valve locked/sealed.
13. Select "BROIL" mode and select the "HI" pressure level. Then, set timer to 10 minutes and press "STOP/START"; it will start the cooking process by building up inside pressure.
14. When the timer goes off, quick release pressure by adjusting the pressure valve to the VENT.
15. After pressure gets released, open the pressure lid.
16. Serve warm and enjoy!

Nutritional Values (Per Serving):
Calories: 653
Fat: 29g
Saturated Fat: 13g
Trans Fat: 0g
Carbohydrates: 43.5g
Fiber: 5g
Sodium: 521mg
Protein: 41g

Chicken Bean Curry

Prep Time: 5-10 min.
Cooking Time: 20 min.
Number of Servings: 6

Ingredients:
4 chicken breasts
½ cup chicken broth
2 cup green beans, cut into halves
2 cups coconut milk
4 tablespoon red curry paste
2 tablespoon lime juice
2 yellow bell pepper, seeded and cut in 2-inch slices
2 red bell pepper, seeded and cut in 2-inch sliced
4 tablespoon sugar
Black pepper and salt to taste

Directions:
1. Take Ninja Foodi multi-cooker, arrange it over a cooking platform, and open the top lid.
2. In the pot, add the chicken, salt, black pepper, red curry paste, coconut milk, broth, and sugar; stir the mixture.
3. Seal the multi-cooker by locking it with the pressure lid; ensure to keep the pressure release valve locked/sealed.
4. Select "PRESSURE" mode and select the "HI" pressure level. Then, set timer to 15 minutes and press "STOP/START"; it will start the cooking process by building up inside pressure.
5. When the timer goes off, quick release pressure by adjusting the pressure valve to the VENT. After pressure gets released, open the pressure lid.
6. Shred the chicken and add back to the cooking pot. Add the bell peppers, green beans, and lime juice; stir the mixture.
7. Seal the multi-cooker by locking it with the crisping lid; ensure to keep the pressure release valve locked/sealed.
8. Select "BROIL" mode and select the "HI" pressure level. Then, set timer to 4 minutes and press "STOP/START"; it will start the cooking process by building up inside pressure.
9. When the timer goes off, quick release pressure by adjusting the pressure valve to the VENT.
10. After pressure gets released, open the pressure lid.
11. Serve warm and enjoy!

Nutritional Values (Per Serving):

Calories: 231

Fat: 4.5g

Saturated Fat: 1g

Trans Fat: 0g

Carbohydrates: 21.5g

Fiber: 4g

Sodium: 527mg

Protein: 25.5g

Turkey Dinner Risotto

Prep Time: 5-10 min.
Cooking Time: 15 min.
Number of Servings: 4

Ingredients:
2 boneless turkey breasts, cut into strips
2 cups chicken broth
1 cup Arborio rice, rinsed and drained
¼ cup chopped fresh parsley
2 lemons, zested and juiced
1 onion, diced
2 garlic cloves, minced
1 tablespoon dried oregano
½ teaspoon sea salt
1 ½ tablespoon olive oil
8 lemon slices
Ground black pepper to taste

Directions:
1. Protein: 47g In a zip-lock bag, add the turkey along with the garlic, oregano, sea salt, juice and zest of two lemons.
2. Shake well to combine and set aside to marinate for 20 minutes.

1. Take Ninja Foodi multi-cooker, arrange it over a cooking platform, and open the top lid.
2. In the pot, add the oil; Select "SEAR/SAUTÉ" mode and select "MD: HI" pressure level.
3. Press "STOP/START." After about 4-5 minutes, the oil will start simmering.
4. Add the onions and cook (while stirring) for 2-3 minutes until they become softened and translucent.
5. Add the rice and chicken broth; season with black pepper and salt to taste.
6. Add the turkey and marinade mixture; stir the mixture.
7. Seal the multi-cooker by locking it with the pressure lid; ensure to keep the pressure release valve locked/sealed.
8. Select "PRESSURE" mode and select the "HI" pressure level. Then, set timer to 12 minutes and press "STOP/START"; it will start the cooking process by building up inside pressure.
9. When the timer goes off, quick release pressure by adjusting the pressure valve to the VENT. After pressure gets released, open the pressure lid.
10. Serve warm with some lemon slices and enjoy!

Nutritional Values (Per Serving):
Calories: 518
Fat: 7g
Saturated Fat: 1.5g
Trans Fat: 0g
Carbohydrates: 29g
Fiber: 6g
Sodium: 483mg
Protein: 47g

Chicken with Wholesome Greens

Prep Time: 5-10 min.
Cooking Time: 14 min.
Number of Servings: 1

Ingredients:
4 ounce chicken breasts, cut into bite-size cubes
1 garlic clove, minced
½ cup baby spinach leaves
3 large kale leaves, chopped
½ cup romaine lettuce, shredded
3 tablespoon olive oil
1 teaspoon balsamic vinegar
Ground black pepper and salt, to taste

Directions:
1. In a mixing bowl, combine the chicken, one tablespoon olive oil, and garlic. Season with ground black pepper and salt to taste. Combine well.
2. Take a baking pan; grease it with some cooking spray, vegetable oil, or butter. In the pan, add the chicken mixture.
3. Take Ninja Foodi multi-cooker, arrange it over a cooking platform, and open the top lid.
4. In the pot, add water and place a reversible rack inside the pot. Place the pan over the rack.
5. Seal the multi-cooker by locking it with the crisping lid; ensure to keep the pressure release valve locked/sealed.
6. Select "BAKE/ROAST" mode and adjust the 390°F temperature level. Then, set timer to 14 minutes and press "STOP/START"; it will start the cooking process by building up inside pressure.
7. When the timer goes off, quick release pressure by adjusting the pressure valve to the VENT. After pressure gets released, open the pressure lid.
8. In another bowl, add the greens. Add the remaining olive oil, balsamic vinegar, salt, and pepper; combine well.
9. Add the chicken mixture and combine; serve warm.

Nutritional Values (Per Serving):
Calories: 346
Fat: 16g
Saturated Fat: 2g
Trans Fat: 0g
Carbohydrates: 20.5g
Fiber: 7g
Sodium: 208mg
Protein: 36g

Chicken with Peach & Tomatoes

Prep Time: 5-10 min.
Cooking Time: 15 min.
Number of Servings: 4

Ingredients:
14 ounces canned diced tomatoes
4 boneless, skinless chicken thighs
2 cloves garlic, minced
15 ounces canned peach chunks, drained
½ teaspoon salt
½ teaspoon cumin
Cheddar cheese, shredded and chopped mint leaves to serve

Directions:
1. Reserve the juice from canned peach chunks; set aside.
2. Take Ninja Foodi multi-cooker, arrange it over a cooking platform, and open the top lid.
3. In the pot, add the chicken, tomatoes, cumin, garlic, 1 cup peach juice, and salt; stir the mixture well.
4. Seal the multi-cooker by locking it with the pressure lid; ensure to keep the pressure release valve locked/sealed.
5. Select "PRESSURE" mode and select the "HI" pressure level. Then, set timer to 15 minutes and press "STOP/START"; it will start the cooking process by building up inside pressure.
6. When the timer goes off, quick release pressure by adjusting the pressure valve to the VENT. After pressure gets released, open the pressure lid.
7. Place the chicken in a separate bowl and shred it. Add to a serving plate.
8. In the pot, add the peach chunks and mix until well combined.
9. Add the peach mixture over the chicken; serve with the mint leaves and shredded cheese on top.

Nutritional Values (Per Serving):
Calories: 234
Fat: 8g
Saturated Fat: 2.5g
Trans Fat: 0g
Carbohydrates: 18g
Fiber: 4g
Sodium: 586mg
Protein: 22g

Chicken Rice with Wholesome Veggies

Prep Time: 10 min.
Cooking Time: 20 min.
Number of Servings: 4

Ingredients:
1 onion, diced
4 garlic cloves, minced
1 tablespoon extra-virgin olive oil
1 pound diced chicken breasts, (boneless, skinless)
2 cups chicken broth
⅛ teaspoon sea salt
⅛ teaspoon freshly ground black pepper
¼ cup soy sauce
1 (16-ounce) bag frozen mixed vegetables
1 cup jasmine rice

Directions:
1. Take Ninja Foodi multi-cooker, arrange it over a cooking platform, and open the top lid.
2. In the pot, add the oil; Select "SEAR/SAUTÉ" mode and select "MD: HI" pressure level.
3. Press "STOP/START." After about 4-5 minutes, the oil will start simmering.
4. Add the onions and cook (while stirring) until they become softened and translucent.
5. Add the garlic and cook until turn fragrant for 1-2 minutes.
6. Add the chicken and season with the salt and pepper — Stir-Cook for 5 minutes to brown the chicken.
7. Add the broth, soy sauce, and rice; stir well.
8. Seal the multi-cooker by locking it with the pressure lid; ensure to keep the pressure release valve locked/sealed.
9. Select "PRESSURE" mode and select the "HI" pressure level. Then, set timer to 3 minutes and press "STOP/START"; it will start the cooking process by building up inside pressure.
10. When the timer goes off, quick release pressure by adjusting the pressure valve to the VENT. After pressure gets released, open the pressure lid.
11. Select "SEAR/SAUTÉ" mode and select the "MD" pressure level; add the vegetables and combine them. Stir-cook for 4-5 minutes.
12. Serve warm and enjoy!

Nutritional Values (Per Serving):

Calories: 429
Fat: 7g
Saturated Fat: 1g
Trans Fat: 0g
Carbohydrates: 49g
Fiber: 8g
Sodium: 1149mg
Protein: 38g

Chicken Carrots with Rice

Prep Time: 10 min.
Cooking Time: 12 min.
Number of Servings: 4

Ingredients:
4 bone-in chicken thighs with skin
1 cup white rice
1 ½ cups chicken broth
2 carrots, peeled and cut into small chunks
2 teaspoons poultry spice
1 teaspoon sea salt
2 tablespoons extra-virgin olive oil
2 teaspoons chopped fresh rosemary

Directions:
1. Take Ninja Foodi multi-cooker, arrange it over a cooking platform, and open the top lid.
2. In the pot, add the stock and rice; place a reversible rack inside the pot. Place the chicken (skin side up) and carrots over the rack.
3. Seal the multi-cooker by locking it with the pressure lid; ensure to keep the pressure release valve locked/sealed.
4. Select "PRESSURE" mode and select the "HI" pressure level. Then, set timer to 2 minutes and press "STOP/START"; it will start the cooking process by building up inside pressure.
5. When the timer goes off, quick release pressure by adjusting the pressure valve to the VENT. After pressure gets released, open the pressure lid.
6. Brush the carrots and chicken with some olive oil. Season the carrots with the rosemary and ½ teaspoon of salt. Season, the chicken with the poultry spice and ½ teaspoon salt.
7. Seal the multi-cooker by locking it with the crisping lid; ensure to keep the pressure release valve locked/sealed.
8. Select "BROIL" mode and select the "HI" pressure level. Then, set timer to 10 minutes and press "STOP/START"; it will start the cooking process by building up inside pressure.
9. When the timer goes off, quick release pressure by adjusting the pressure valve to the VENT.
10. After pressure gets released, open the pressure lid.
11. Serve warm and enjoy!

Nutritional Values (Per Serving):
Calories: 413
Fat: 17g
Saturated Fat: 4g
Trans Fat: 0g
Carbohydrates: 38g
Fiber: 6g
Sodium: 681mg

Protein: 17g

Creamy Chicken Delight

Prep Time: 10 min.
Cooking Time: 15 min.
Number of Servings: 4

Ingredients:
1 pound chicken breasts
½ cup sour cream
1 small onion
2 tablespoons butter, melted
Salt to taste

Directions:
1. Season the chicken with salt, black pepper.
2. Take Ninja Foodi multi-cooker, arrange it over a cooking platform, and open the top lid.
3. In the pot, add the butter; Select "SEAR/SAUTÉ" mode and select "MD: HI" pressure level.
4. Press "STOP/START." After about 4-5 minutes, the butter will start simmering.
5. Add the onions and cook (while stirring) for 2-3 minutes until they become softened and translucent. Add the chicken breasts.
6. Seal the multi-cooker by locking it with the pressure lid; ensure to keep the pressure release valve locked/sealed.
7. Select "PRESSURE" mode and select the "HI" pressure level. Then, set timer to 10 minutes and press "STOP/START"; it will start the cooking process by building up inside pressure.
8. When the timer goes off, quick release pressure by adjusting the pressure valve to the VENT. After pressure gets released, open the pressure lid.
9. Select "SEAR/SAUTÉ" mode and select the "MD" pressure level; add the cream and combine. Stir-cook for 4 minutes.
10. Serve warm and enjoy!

Nutritional Values (Per Serving):
Calories: 426
Fat: 24g
Saturated Fat: 11g
Trans Fat: 0g
Carbohydrates: 9g
Fiber: 1g
Sodium: 247mg
Protein: 44.5g

Beer-Braised Chicken Wings

Prep Time: 10-15 min.
Cooking Time: 40 min.
Number of Servings: 2
Ingredients:
1 tablespoon garlic powder
1/2 cup BBQ sauce
2 tablespoons canola oil
1/2 cup beer
1 pound chicken wings
Salt and ground black pepper to taste
Directions:

1. In a mixing bowl, add the chicken wings and other ingredients. Combine well.
2. Take Ninja Foodi Grill, arrange it over your kitchen platform, and open the top lid. Arrange the grill grate and close the top lid.
3. Press "GRILL" and select the "MED" grill function. Adjust the timer to 25 minutes and then press "START/STOP." Ninja Foodi will start preheating.
4. Ninja Foodi is preheated and ready to cook when it starts to beep. After you hear a beep, open the top lid.
5. Arrange the chicken wings over the grill grate. Reserve the marinade.
6. Close the top lid and cook for 13 minutes. Now open the top lid, flip the chicken. Close the top lid and cook for 12 more minutes.
7. Take out the grill plate and set aside the cooked chicken.
8. In the pot, add the marinade. Press "ROAST" and adjust the temperature to 350°F. Adjust the timer to 15 minutes and then press "START/STOP."
9. Close the top lid and allow it to cook until the timer reads zero. Serve the chicken wings with the hot sauce.

Nutritional Values (Per Serving):
Calories: 546
Fat: 27g
Saturated Fat: 8.5g
Trans Fat: 0g
Carbohydrates: 19g
Fiber: 3.5g
Sodium: 448mg
Protein: 57g

Chicken Pineapple Kebabs

Prep Time: 5-10 min.
Cooking Time: 14 min.
Number of Servings: 4
Ingredients:
1 cup teriyaki sauce
1 pound chicken breasts (boneless, skinless), cut into 2-inch cubes
2 green bell peppers, seeded and cut into 1-inch cubes
2 cups pineapple, cut into 1-inch cubes
Directions:
1. Take a zip-lock bag, add ½ cup teriyaki sauce and chicken. Shake well and refrigerate for 30 minutes to marinate.
2. Take Ninja Foodi Grill, arrange it over your kitchen platform, and open the top lid.
3. Arrange the grill grate and close the top lid.
4. Press "GRILL" and select the "MED" grill function. Adjust the timer to 14 minutes and then press "START/STOP." Ninja Foodi will start preheating.
5. Take the skewers, thread the chicken, pineapple, and peppers. Thread alternatively.
6. Ninja Foodi is preheated and ready to cook when it starts to beep. After you hear a beep, open the top lid.
7. Arrange the skewers over the grill grate — Reserve marinade.
8. Close the top lid and allow it to cook until the timer reads zero. Baste the skewers in between with the remaining teriyaki sauce. Cook until the food thermometer reaches 165°F for chicken.
9. Serve warm.

Nutritional Values (Per Serving):
Calories: 246
Fat: 4g
Saturated Fat: 0g
Trans Fat: 0g
Carbohydrates: 24.5g
Fiber: 3g
Sodium: 1743mg
Protein: 28g

Garlic Orange Chicken

Prep Time: 5-10 min.
Cooking Time: 22 min.
Number of Servings: 4
Ingredients:
4 chicken breasts, bones removed
4 tablespoons olive oil
4 cloves garlic, minced
4 ounces orange juice
1 tablespoon vinegar
2 teaspoon turmeric powder
2 teaspoons oregano
½ teaspoon chili powder
Directions:
1. In a mixing bowl, add the ingredients. Combine well.
2. Refrigerate for 2-3 hours to marinate.
3. Take Ninja Foodi Grill, arrange it over your kitchen platform, and open the top lid.
4. Arrange the grill grate and close the top lid.
5. Press "GRILL" and select the "MED" grill function. Adjust the timer to 22 minutes and then press "START/STOP." Ninja Foodi will start preheating.
6. Ninja Foodi is preheated and ready to cook when it starts to beep. After you hear a beep, open the top lid.
7. Arrange the chicken over the grill grate.
8. Close the top lid and cook for 11 minutes. Now open the top lid, flip the chicken.
9. Close the top lid and cook for 11 more minutes. Serve warm.

Nutritional Values (Per Serving):
Calories: 586
Fat: 37.5g
Saturated Fat: 9g
Trans Fat: 0g
Carbohydrates: 11.5g
Fiber: 2g
Sodium: 358mg
Protein: 59g

Italian Turkey Roast

Prep Time: 5-10 min.
Cooking Time: 50 min.
Number of Servings: 5-6
Ingredients:
1 teaspoon paprika
1 teaspoon Italian seasoning
1 (3 pound) turkey breasts, with skin
1/4 cup butter, melted
1 clove garlic, minced
1/2 teaspoon herb seasoning blend
Salt and ground black pepper to taste
1 teaspoon shallot, minced
Directions:
1. In a safe microwave bowl, add the butter, garlic, shallot, and other seasonings and shallot. Microwave for 1 minute. Coat the turkey with half the butter mixture.
2. Take Ninja Foodi Grill, arrange it over your kitchen platform, and open the top lid. Lightly grease cooking pot with some oil or cooking spray.
3. Press "ROAST" and adjust the temperature to 400°F. Adjust the timer to 25 minutes and then press "START/STOP." Ninja Foodi will start preheating.
4. Ninja Foodi is preheated and ready to cook when it starts to beep. After you hear a beep, open the top lid.
5. Arrange the turkey directly inside the pot. Close the top lid and allow it to cook until the timer reads zero.
6. Open the lid and brush the turkey with remaining butter. Close the top lid and allow it to cook until the timer reads zero.
7. Open the lid and brush the turkey with remaining butter.
8. Press "ROAST" and adjust the temperature to 390°F. Adjust the timer to 10 minutes and then press "START/STOP."
9. Close the top lid and allow it to cook until the timer reads zero. Serve warm.

Nutritional Values (Per Serving):
Calories: 402
Fat: 13.5g
Saturated Fat: 5g
Trans Fat: 0g
Carbohydrates: 9g
Fiber: 1g
Sodium: 425mg
Protein: 56.5g

Chicken Crisped Cutlets

Prep Time: 5-10 min.
Cooking Time: 22 min.
Number of Servings: 2
Ingredients:
2 large eggs
½ cup all-purpose flour
2 boneless, skinless chicken breasts
4 tablespoons butter, melted
½ teaspoon black pepper
Juice of 1 lemon
1 tablespoon capers, drained
Directions:

1. In a mixing bowl, whisk the eggs. Combine well. In another mixing bowl, add the flour and black pepper. Combine well.
2. Coat the chicken with the flour and then coat with the egg mixture and then again coat with the flour mixture.
3. Take Ninja Foodi Grill, arrange it over your kitchen platform, and open the top lid. Arrange the Crisping Basket inside the pot.
4. Press "AIR CRISP" and adjust the temperature to 375°F. Adjust the timer to 22 minutes and then press "START/STOP." Ninja Foodi will start preheating.
5. Ninja Foodi is preheated and ready to cook when it starts to beep. After you hear a beep, open the top lid.
6. Arrange the chicken directly inside the basket.
7. Close the top lid and cook for 18 minutes. After 18 minutes, shake the basket and close the top lid and cook for another 4 minutes.
8. In a saucepan, melt the butter. Add the capers and lemon juice; stir-cook for 3-4 minutes.
9. Serve the chicken with the butter sauce on top.

Nutritional Values (Per Serving):
Calories: 493
Fat: 26.5g
Saturated Fat: 13g
Trans Fat: 0g
Carbohydrates: 27g
Fiber: 2.5g
Sodium: 459mg
Protein: 35g

Classic Pork Meal with Green Bean

Prep Time: 5-10 min.
Cooking Time: 25 min.
Number of Servings: 4

Ingredients:
2 pounds pork stew meat, cut into small cubes
1 tablespoon avocado oil
1 pound green beans, trimmed and halved
2 minced garlic cloves
1 tablespoon basil, chopped
1 teaspoon chili powder
¾ cup veggie stock
A pinch of black pepper and salt

Directions:
1. Take Ninja Foodi multi-cooker, arrange it over a cooking platform, and open the top lid.
2. In the pot, add the oil; Select "SEAR/SAUTÉ" mode and select "MD: HI" pressure level.
3. Press "STOP/START." After about 4-5 minutes, the oil will start simmering.
4. Add the meat, garlic, and stir-cook for about 4-5 minutes to brown evenly.
5. Add the remaining ingredients; stir well.
6. Seal the multi-cooker by locking it with the pressure lid; ensure to keep the pressure release valve locked/sealed.
7. Select "PRESSURE" mode and select the "HI" pressure level. Then, set timer to 20 minutes and press "STOP/START"; it will start the cooking process by building up inside pressure.
8. When the timer goes off, naturally release inside pressure for about 8-10 minutes. Then, quick-release pressure by adjusting the pressure valve to the VENT.
9. After pressure gets released, open the pressure lid.
10. Serve warm.

Nutritional Values (Per Serving):

Calories: 403
Fat: 15.5g
Saturated Fat: 2g
Trans Fat: 0g
Carbohydrates: 18g
Fiber: 4g
Sodium: 624mg
Protein: 53.5g

BBQ Beer Ribs

Prep Time: 5-10 min.
Cooking Time: 25 min.
Number of Servings: 4

Ingredients:
1 (around 2-3 pound) rack baby back ribs, cut into quarters
1 cup beer of your choice
3 tablespoons brown sugar
1 tablespoon sea salt
1 tablespoon black pepper
1 ½ tablespoons smoked paprika
2 teaspoons garlic powder
1 cup barbecue sauce

Directions:
1. In a mixing bowl, add the brown sugar, salt, black pepper, paprika, and garlic powder; combine well.
2. Season the ribs evenly with the seasoning mix.
3. Take Ninja Foodi multi-cooker, arrange it over a cooking platform, and open the top lid.
4. In the pot, add the beer and arrange reversible rack; place the Crisping Basket over the rack.
5. In the basket, add the seasoned ribs.
6. Seal the multi-cooker by locking it with the pressure lid; ensure to keep the pressure release valve locked/sealed.
7. Select "PRESSURE" mode and select the "HI" pressure level. Then, set timer to 10 minutes and press "STOP/START"; it will start the cooking process by building up inside pressure.
8. When the timer goes off, quick release pressure by adjusting the pressure valve to the VENT. After pressure gets released, open the pressure lid.
9. Set aside the pressure lid.
10. Seal the multi-cooker by locking it with the crisping lid; ensure to keep the pressure release valve locked/sealed.
11. Select the "AIR CRISP" mode and adjust the 400°F temperature level. Then, set timer to 15 minutes and press "STOP/START"; it will start the cooking process by building up inside pressure.
12. Cook for 10 minutes; open the lid and crush the ribs with the barbeque sauce. Close lid and cook for 5 minutes.
13. When the timer goes off, quick release pressure by adjusting the pressure valve to the VENT.
14. After pressure gets released, open the pressure lid.
15. Serve warm and enjoy!

Nutritional Values (Per Serving):

Calories: 743

Fat: 46.5g

Saturated Fat: 14g

Trans Fat: 0g

Carbohydrates: 39g

Fiber: 2.5g

Sodium: 1846mg

Protein: 38g

Wholesome Asparagus Beef

Prep Time: 5-10 min.
Cooking Time: 28 min.
Number of Servings: 4

Ingredients:
1 pound beef stew meat, cut into cubes
2 tablespoons grated ginger
1 cup tomato puree
A pinch of black pepper and salt
½ pound asparagus, trimmed, steamed and halved
1 yellow onion, chopped
1 tablespoon olive oil

Directions:
1. Take Ninja Foodi multi-cooker, arrange it over a cooking platform, and open the top lid.
2. In the pot, add the oil; Select "SEAR/SAUTÉ" mode and select "MD: HI" pressure level.
3. Press "STOP/START." After about 4-5 minutes, the oil will start simmering.
4. Add the meat and stir cook for about 5 minutes to brown evenly.
5. Add the onion, ginger, black pepper, and salt; cook, while stirring, for 4 minutes more. Add the tomato puree; stir the mixture.
6. Seal the multi-cooker by locking it with the pressure lid; ensure to keep the pressure release valve locked/sealed.
7. Select "PRESSURE" mode and select the "HI" pressure level. Then, set timer to 15 minutes and press "STOP/START"; it will start the cooking process by building up inside pressure.
8. When the timer goes off, naturally release inside pressure for about 8-10 minutes. Then, quick-release pressure by adjusting the pressure valve to the VENT.
9. After pressure gets released, open the pressure lid.
10. Select "SEAR/SAUTÉ" mode and select the "MD" pressure level; add the asparagus and combine. Stir-cook for 4 minutes.
11. Serve warm and enjoy!

Nutritional Values (Per Serving):

Calories: 243

Fat: 10.5g

Saturated Fat: 3g

Trans Fat: 0g

Carbohydrates: 10g

Fiber: 3g

Sodium: 824mg

Protein: 35g

Broccoli Pork with Rice

Prep Time: 5-10 min.
Cooking Time: 14 min.
Number of Servings: 4

Ingredients:
1 head broccoli, cut into florets
1 tablespoon extra-virgin olive oil
¼ teaspoon black pepper
¼ teaspoon sea salt
1 cup long-grain white rice
1 cup water
1 trimmed pork tenderloin, cut into 1-inch pieces
1 cup teriyaki sauce
Sesame seeds to garnish

Directions:
1. In a mixing bowl, combine the broccoli with the olive oil. Season with the ground black pepper and salt.
2. In another bowl, combine the sauce and pork until evenly coated.
3. Take Ninja Foodi multi-cooker, arrange it over a cooking platform, and open the top lid.
4. In the pot, add the water and rice.
5. Seal the multi-cooker by locking it with the pressure lid; ensure to keep the pressure release valve locked/sealed.
6. Select "PRESSURE" mode and select the "HI" pressure level. Then, set timer to 2 minutes and press "STOP/START"; it will start the cooking process by building up inside pressure.
7. When the timer goes off, quick release pressure by adjusting the pressure valve to the VENT. After pressure gets released, open the pressure lid.
8. Over the rice, arrange the reversible rack and place the pork and broccoli over the rack.
9. Seal the multi-cooker by locking it with the crisping lid; ensure to keep the pressure release valve locked/sealed.
10. Select "BROIL" mode and select the "HI" pressure level. Then, set timer to 12 minutes and press "STOP/START"; it will start the cooking process by building up inside pressure.
11. When the timer goes off, quick release pressure by adjusting the pressure valve to the VENT.
12. After pressure gets released, open the pressure lid.
13. Serve the pork mixture warm with the cooked rice and some sesame seeds on top.

Nutritional Values (Per Serving):

Calories: 453
Fat: 9.5g
Saturated Fat: 1.5g
Trans Fat: 0g
Carbohydrates: 52g
Fiber: 5.5g
Sodium: 1420mg
Protein: 39g

Lamb Chickpeas Tomato

Prep Time: 5-10 min.
Cooking Time: 25 min.
Number of Servings: 4

Ingredients:
2 red onions, sliced
1 cup chicken stock
1 pound lamb steaks, cut into cubes
10 ounces canned tomatoes, chopped
10 ounces canned chickpeas, drained
2 garlic cloves, minced
2 teaspoons hot paprika
2 teaspoons honey

Directions:
1. Take a baking pan; grease it with some cooking spray, vegetable oil, or butter.
2. Take Ninja Foodi multi-cooker, arrange it over a cooking platform, and open the top lid.
3. In the pot, add water and place a reversible rack inside the pot. Place the pan over the rack.
4. In the pan, add the stock, lamb and other ingredients; stir gently.
5. Seal the multi-cooker by locking it with the crisping lid; ensure to keep the pressure release valve locked/sealed.
6. Select "BAKE/ROAST" mode and adjust the 380°F temperature level. Then, set timer to 25 minutes and press "STOP/START"; it will start the cooking process by building up inside pressure.
7. When the timer goes off, quick release pressure by adjusting the pressure valve to the VENT. After pressure gets released, open the pressure lid.
8. Serve warm and enjoy!

Nutritional Values (Per Serving):
Calories: 357
Fat: 12g
Saturated Fat: 4g
Trans Fat: 0g
Carbohydrates: 25g
Fiber: 4.5g
Sodium: 741mg
Protein: 47g

Smoked Sausage with Egg Noodles

Prep Time: 5-10 min.
Cooking Time: 20 min.
Number of Servings: 4

Ingredients:
3 slices bacon, diced
1 small onion, sliced
⅓ cup dry white wine
4 cups shredded cabbage or coleslaw mix
1 ½ pounds kielbasa or your choice of smoked sausage, cut into 4 pieces
1 cup chicken stock or broth
1 teaspoon kosher salt
¼ teaspoon black pepper
5 ounces wide egg noodles

Directions:
1. Take Ninja Foodi multi-cooker, arrange it over a cooking platform, and open the top lid.
2. Select "SEAR/SAUTÉ" mode and select "MD:HI" pressure level.
3. Press "STOP/START." After about 4-5 minutes, the oil will start simmering.
4. In the pot, add the bacon and cook for 2-3 minutes per side until turn crispy and fat is rendered.
5. Keep the fat inside and place the bacon over some paper towels.
6. In the pot, sauté the onion with the fat until it becomes softened and translucent.
7. Add the wine and keep cooking until reduced in quantity.
8. Add the chicken stock, salt, and noodles; stir the mixture. Add the cabbage and sausage on top.
9. Seal the multi-cooker by locking it with the pressure lid; ensure to keep the pressure release valve locked/sealed.
10. Select "PRESSURE" mode and select the "HI" pressure level. Then, set timer to 3 minutes and press "STOP/START"; it will start the cooking process by building up inside pressure.
11. When the timer goes off, quick release pressure by adjusting the pressure valve to the VENT. After pressure gets released, open the pressure lid.
12. In the pot, arrange a reversible rack and place the sausage over the rack.
13. Seal the multi-cooker by locking it with the crisping lid; ensure to keep the pressure release valve locked/sealed.
14. Select "BAKE/ROAST" mode and adjust the 390°F temperature level. Then, set timer to 8 minutes and press "STOP/START"; it will start the cooking process by building up inside pressure.

15. When the timer goes off, quick release pressure by adjusting the pressure valve to the VENT. After pressure gets released, open the pressure lid.
16. Take out the cooked noodle mixture and add the sausage on top; stir and add the bacon on top. Serve warm.

Nutritional Values (Per Serving):
Calories: 623
Fat: 36.5g
Saturated Fat: 12g
Trans Fat: 0g
Carbohydrates: 41g
Fiber: 3.5g
Sodium: 1624mg
Protein: 33g

Healthy Broccoli Beef Dinner

Prep Time: 5-10 min.
Cooking Time: 20 min.
Number of Servings: 4

Ingredients:
4 garlic cloves, minced
½ cup soy sauce
1 tablespoon extra-virgin olive oil
2 pounds flank steak, cut into thin strips
½ cup + 3 tablespoons water
½ teaspoon minced ginger
⅔ cup dark brown sugar
2 tablespoons cornstarch
1 head broccoli, trimmed and cut into florets
3 scallions, thinly sliced

Directions:
1. Take Ninja Foodi multi-cooker, arrange it over a cooking platform, and open the top lid.
2. In the pot, add the oil; Select "SEAR/SAUTÉ" mode and select "MD: HI" pressure level.
3. Press "STOP/START." After about 4-5 minutes, the oil will start simmering.
4. Add the beef strips and stir cook for about 4-5 minutes to brown evenly. Remove from the pot and set aside.
5. Add the garlic and sauté for 1 minute. Add the soy sauce, ½ cup of water, ginger, and brown sugar. Stir the mixture and add the beef; combine again.
6. Seal the multi-cooker by locking it with the pressure lid; ensure to keep the pressure release valve locked/sealed.
7. Select "PRESSURE" mode and select the "HI" pressure level. Then, set timer to 10 minutes and press "STOP/START"; it will start the cooking process by building up inside pressure.
8. When the timer goes off, quick release pressure by adjusting the pressure valve to the VENT. After pressure gets released, open the pressure lid.
9. In a mixing bowl, add the cornstarch and the remaining three tablespoons of water. Whisk to combine well.
10. Select "SEAR/SAUTÉ" mode and select the "MD" pressure level; add the cornstarch mixture and combine it. Stir-cook until simmers.
11. Serve warm with the scallions on top and enjoy!

Nutritional Values (Per Serving):
Calories: 516
Fat: 16.5g
Saturated Fat: 6g
Trans Fat: 0g
Carbohydrates: 48g
Fiber: 5.5g
Sodium: 1854mg
Protein: 59g

Tangy Pork Carnitas

Prep Time: 10 min.
Cooking Time: 25 min.
Number of Servings: 5-6

Ingredients:
2 pounds pork shoulder, bone-in
2 tablespoons butter, melted
2 oranges, juiced
Ground black pepper and salt to taste
1 teaspoon garlic powder
5-6 warmed carnitas

Directions:
1. Season the pork with salt, garlic powder, and black pepper.
2. Take Ninja Foodi multi-cooker, arrange it over a cooking platform, and open the top lid.
3. In the pot, add the butter; Select "SEAR/SAUTÉ" mode and select "MD: HI" pressure level.
4. Press "STOP/START." After about 4-5 minutes, the butter will start simmering.
5. Add the meat and stir cook for about 2-3 minutes to brown evenly. Stir in orange juice.
6. Seal the multi-cooker by locking it with the pressure lid; ensure to keep the pressure release valve locked/sealed.
7. Select "PRESSURE" mode and select the "HI" pressure level. Then, set timer to 15 minutes and press "STOP/START"; it will start the cooking process by building up inside pressure.
8. When the timer goes off, naturally release inside pressure for about 8-10 minutes. Then, quick-release pressure by adjusting the pressure valve to the VENT.
9. Select "BROIL" mode and select the "HI" pressure level. Then, set timer to 15 minutes and press "STOP/START"; it will start the cooking process by building up inside pressure.
10. When the timer goes off, quick release pressure by adjusting the pressure valve to the VENT.
11. After pressure gets released, open the pressure lid.
12. Shred the meat and remove the bones. Add the mixture over the carnitas; fold and serve warm.

Nutritional Values (Per Serving):
Calories: 486
Fat: 32g
Saturated Fat: 12.5g
Trans Fat: 0g
Carbohydrates: 9g
Fiber: 2g
Sodium: 203mg
Protein: 34g

Spinach Beef Casserole

Prep Time: 10 min.
Cooking Time: 70 min.
Number of Servings: 6-7

Ingredients:
¼ cup tomato ketchup
1 pound lean ground beef, grass-fed
½ cup onion, chopped
2 garlic cloves, minced
1 cup cheddar cheese, grated
½ cup green bell pepper, seeded and chopped
2 medium eggs, beaten
3 cups fresh spinach, chopped
1 teaspoon dried thyme, crushed
6 cups mozzarella cheese, freshly grated
Black pepper to taste

Directions:
1. Take a mixing bowl and add all ingredients except spinach and cheese. Combine well.
2. Place a wax paper over a kitchen surface; add the meat over and top it with cheese, spinach. Roll the paper to form a meatloaf. Remove wax paper.
3. Take Ninja Foodi multi-cooker, arrange it over a cooking platform, and open the top lid.
4. In the pot, add water and place a reversible rack inside the pot. Place the baking pan over the rack. Add the meatloaf in the pan.
5. Seal the multi-cooker by locking it with the crisping lid; ensure to keep the pressure release valve locked/sealed.
6. Select "BAKE/ROAST" mode and adjust the 380°F temperature level. Then, set timer to 70 minutes and press "STOP/START"; it will start the cooking process by building up inside pressure.
7. When the timer goes off, quick release pressure by adjusting the pressure valve to the VENT. After pressure gets released, open the pressure lid.
8. Serve warm and enjoy!

Nutritional Values (Per Serving):
Calories: 303
Fat: 14g
Saturated Fat: 6.5g
Trans Fat: 0g
Carbohydrates: 15.5g
Fiber: 3g
Sodium: 357mg
Protein: 19g

Rosemary Lamb Shanks

Prep Time: 10 min.
Cooking Time: 35-40 min.
Number of Servings: 4

Ingredients:
2 tablespoons extra-virgin olive oil
1 onion, chopped
2 carrots, chopped
4 garlic cloves, minced
2 lamb shanks
½ teaspoon sea salt
½ teaspoon black pepper, freshly ground
1 (14-ounce) can diced tomatoes, undrained
2 celery stalks, chopped
3 ½ cups beef broth
2 rosemary sprigs

Directions:
1. Season the lamb shanks with the salt and black pepper.
2. Take Ninja Foodi multi-cooker, arrange it over a cooking platform, and open the top lid.
3. In the pot, add one tablespoon oil; Select "SEAR/SAUTÉ" mode and select "MD: HI" pressure level.
4. Press "STOP/START." After about 4-5 minutes, the oil will start simmering.
5. Add the lamb shanks and stir-cook for about 8-10 minutes to brown evenly. Set aside the lamb shanks.
6. In the pot, add the remaining one tablespoon of oil.
7. Add the onions, garlic, and cook (while stirring) for 4-5 minutes until they become softened and translucent.
8. Add the carrots and celery and cook for 3 minutes more.
9. Add the tomatoes, broth, and rosemary; stir and add the lamb shanks.
10. Seal the multi-cooker by locking it with the pressure lid; ensure to keep the pressure release valve locked/sealed.
11. Select "PRESSURE" mode and select the "HI" pressure level. Then, set timer to 30 minutes and press "STOP/START"; it will start the cooking process by building up inside pressure.
12. When the timer goes off, quick release pressure by adjusting the pressure valve to the VENT. After pressure gets released, open the pressure lid.
13. Shred the lamb; serve warm and enjoy!

Nutritional Values (Per Serving):

Calories: 698
Fat: 32.5g
Saturated Fat: 14g
Trans Fat: 0g
Carbohydrates: 18g
Fiber: 4g
Sodium: 854mg
Protein: 56.5g

Classic Mustard Pork Chops

Prep Time: 5-10 min.
Cooking Time: 30 min.
Number of Servings: 4

Ingredients:
2 tablespoons butter
4 pork chops
2 tablespoons Dijon mustard
Ground black pepper and salt to taste
1 tablespoon fresh rosemary, coarsely chopped

Directions:
1. Marinate the pork chops with the mustard, rosemary, salt, pepper in a bowl for 2-3 hours.
2. Take Ninja Foodi multi-cooker, arrange it over a cooking platform, and open the top lid.
3. In the pot, add the butter and pork chops.
4. Seal the multi-cooker by locking it with the pressure lid; ensure to keep the pressure release valve locked/sealed.
5. Select "PRESSURE" mode and select the "LO: MD" pressure level. Then, set timer to 30 minutes and press "STOP/START"; it will start the cooking process by building up inside pressure.
6. When the timer goes off, naturally release inside pressure for about 8-10 minutes. Then, quick-release pressure by adjusting the pressure valve to the VENT.
7. Serve warm and enjoy!

Nutritional Values (Per Serving):
Calories: 308
Fat: 25g
Saturated Fat: 11g
Trans Fat: 0g
Carbohydrates: 5g
Fiber: 0.5g
Sodium: 254mg
Protein: 19g

Beef Congee with Kale

Prep Time: 5-10 min.
Cooking Time: 30 min.
Number of Servings: 6

Ingredients:
2 pounds ground beef
1-inch piece ginger, minced
2 cloves garlic, minced
6 cups beef stock
1 cup kale, roughly chopped
1 cup jasmine rice, uncooked, rinsed and drained
1 cups water
Ground black pepper and salt to taste
Fresh cilantro, chopped

Directions:
1. Take Ninja Foodi multi-cooker, arrange it over a cooking platform, and open the top lid.
2. In the pot, add the garlic, rice, and ginger.
3. Add the stock and water. Stir the mixture and add the beef.
4. Seal the multi-cooker by locking it with the pressure lid; ensure to keep the pressure release valve locked/sealed.
5. Select "PRESSURE" mode and select the "HI" pressure level. Then, set timer to 30 minutes and press "STOP/START"; it will start the cooking process by building up inside pressure.
6. When the timer goes off, quick release pressure by adjusting the pressure valve to the VENT. After pressure gets released, open the pressure lid.
7. Stir in the kale. Add pepper and salt for seasoning. Serve warm with some cilantro on top and enjoy!

Nutritional Values (Per Serving):
Calories: 328
Fat: 15g
Saturated Fat: 4g
Trans Fat: 0g
Carbohydrates: 12g
Fiber: 2g
Sodium: 658mg
Protein: 37g

Beef Pasta Mania

Prep Time: 5-10 min.
Cooking Time: 10 min.
Number of Servings: 4

Ingredients:
1 tablespoon extra-virgin olive oil
2 pounds beef, ground
1 cup water
1 cup dry red wine
2 (24-ounce) jars marinara sauce
1 (16-ounce) pack ziti pasta
½ teaspoon sea salt
½ teaspoon garlic powder
1 cup shredded mozzarella cheese
1 cup ricotta cheese
½ cup chopped fresh parsley

Directions:
1. Take Ninja Foodi multi-cooker, arrange it over a cooking platform, and open the top lid.
2. In the pot, add the oil; Select "SEAR/SAUTÉ" mode and select "MD: HI" pressure level.
3. Press "STOP/START." After about 4-5 minutes, the oil will start simmering.
4. Add the beef and stir cook for about 6-8 minutes to brown evenly.
5. Add the marinara sauce, water, wine, and pasts; stir and season with the garlic powder and salt.
6. Seal the multi-cooker by locking it with the pressure lid; ensure to keep the pressure release valve locked/sealed.
7. Select "PRESSURE" mode and select the "LO" pressure level. Then, set timer to 2 minutes and press "STOP/START"; it will start the cooking process by building up inside pressure.
8. When the timer goes off, naturally release inside pressure for about 8-10 minutes. Then, quick-release pressure by adjusting the pressure valve to the VENT.
9. Stir in the ricotta and mozzarella cheese.
10. Seal the multi-cooker by locking it with the crisping lid; ensure to keep the pressure release valve locked/sealed.
11. Select "BROIL" mode and select the "HI" pressure level. Then, set timer to 3 minutes and press "STOP/START"; it will start the cooking process by building up inside pressure.
12. When the timer goes off, quick release pressure by adjusting the pressure valve to the VENT.
13. After pressure gets released, open the pressure lid.
14. Serve warm with some parsley on top and enjoy!

Nutritional Values (Per Serving):

Calories: 741
Fat: 31.5g
Saturated Fat: 16g
Trans Fat: 0g
Carbohydrates: 52.5g
Fiber: 8.5g
Sodium: 1258mg
Protein: 57g

Mexican Citrus Steak

Prep Time: 5-10 min.
Cooking Time: 8 min.
Number of Servings: 2
Ingredients:
2 pound flank steak
1 onion, sliced into rings
1 teaspoon cumin
1 cup orange juice
2 limes, squeezed and zested
2 teaspoons Mexico or regular chili powder
3 teaspoons sea salt
Warm tacos or tortillas to serve
Filling: Shredded lettuce, cheese, and sweet or chili sauce (optional)
Directions:
1. Take a zip-lock bag, add all the ingredients. Shake well and refrigerate for 3-4 hours to marinate.
2. Take Ninja Foodi Grill, arrange it over your kitchen platform, and open the top lid.
3. Arrange the grill grate and close the top lid.
4. Press "GRILL" and select the "HIGH" grill function. Adjust the timer to 8 minutes and then press "START/STOP." Ninja Foodi will start preheating.
5. Ninja Foodi is preheated and ready to cook when it starts to beep. After you hear a beep, open the top lid.
6. Arrange the steak over the grill grate.
7. Close the top lid and cook for 4 minutes. Now open the top lid, flip the steaks.
8. Close the top lid and cook for four more minutes. Slice the steak thinly.
9. Arrange the tacos or tortillas, add sliced steak, and add filling ingredients as you like. Serve warm.

Nutritional Values (Per Serving):
Calories: 687
Fat: 19g
Saturated Fat: 8.5g
Trans Fat: 0g
Carbohydrates: 21g
Fiber: 2g
Sodium: 1864mg
Protein: 56g

Seasoned Pork Ribs

Prep Time: 5-10 min.
Cooking Time: 25 min.
Number of Servings: 2
Ingredients:
½ teaspoon mustard
2 ¼ pounds pork spareribs
1 tablespoon paprika
1 teaspoon garlic powder
1 tablespoons salt
1 tablespoon brown sugar
1 teaspoon onion powder
1 teaspoon pork & poultry seasoning
Directions:
1. In a mixing bowl, add all the ingredients. Combine the ingredients to mix well with each other.
2. Take Ninja Foodi Grill, arrange it over your kitchen platform, and open the top lid.
3. Arrange the grill grate and close the top lid.
4. Press "GRILL" and select the "MED" grill function. Adjust the timer to 25 minutes and then press "START/STOP." Ninja Foodi will start preheating.
5. Ninja Foodi is preheated and ready to cook when it starts to beep. After you hear a beep, open the top lid.
6. Arrange the ribs over the grill grate.
7. Close the top lid and cook for 13 minutes. Now open the top lid, flip the ribs.
8. Close the top lid and cook for 12 more minutes.
9. Serve warm.

Nutritional Values (Per Serving):
Calories: 592
Fat: 26g
Saturated Fat: 7g
Trans Fat: 0g
Carbohydrates: 9g
Fiber: 2g
Sodium: 526mg
Protein: 61g

Couscous Lamb Meal

Prep Time: 5-10 min.
Cooking Time: 16 min.
Number of Servings: 6-8
Ingredients:
Juice of 2 lemons
1 1/2 cup yogurt
Salt to taste
2 garlic cloves, minced
1 (10 ounce) pack couscous
1 tablespoon and 1 teaspoon cumin
1 1/2 pound lamb leg, boneless, cut into cubes
Ground black pepper to taste
3 tablespoon olive oil
1/2 cucumber, seeded and diced
2 tomatoes, seeded and diced
1/2 small red onion, finely chopped
1/4 cup finely chopped fresh mint
1/4 cup finely chopped fresh parsley
Lemon wedges
Directions:

1. In a mixing bowl, whisk the yogurt, garlic, cumin, lemon juice, salt, and black pepper. Combine well. Add the lamb and coat well.
2. Cook the couscous as per pack instructions and fluff.
3. In a mixing bowl, add the red onion with cucumber, tomatoes, parsley, mint, lemon juice, olive oil, salt, and couscous. Combine well.
4. Take 8 skewers, thread the lamb. Season with black pepper and salt.
5. Take Ninja Foodi Grill, arrange it over your kitchen platform, and open the top lid. Arrange the grill grate and close the top lid.
6. Press "GRILL" and select the "HIGH" grill function. Adjust the timer to 8 minutes and then press "START/STOP." Ninja Foodi will start preheating.
7. Ninja Foodi is preheated and ready to cook when it starts to beep. After you hear a beep, open the top lid.
8. Arrange the half skewers over the grill grate. Close the top lid and cook for 4 minutes. Now open the top lid, flip the skewers.
9. Close the top lid and cook for 4 more minutes.
10. Repeat with remaining skewers. Serve the grilled meat with the couscous mixture.

Nutritional Values (Per Serving):

Calories: 436
Fat: 11g
Saturated Fat: 4.5g
Trans Fat: 0g
Carbohydrates: 20g
Fiber: 3g
Sodium: 658mg
Protein: 17.5g

Spiced Grilled Steak

Prep Time: 5-10 min.
Cooking Time: 8 min.
Number of Servings: 2
Ingredients:
2 (8-ounce) flank steaks
2 teaspoons ground cumin
1 teaspoon sea salt
1 tablespoon chili powder
1 teaspoon dried oregano
¼ teaspoon ground black pepper
Directions:
1. In a mixing bowl, add the chili powder, oregano, cumin, salt, and pepper. Combine well.
2. Season the steak with the prepared mixture.
3. Take Ninja Foodi Grill, arrange it over your kitchen platform, and open the top lid.
4. Arrange the grill grate and close the top lid.
5. Press "GRILL" and select the "HIGH" grill function. Adjust the timer to 8 minutes and then press "START/STOP." Ninja Foodi will start preheating.
6. Ninja Foodi is preheated and ready to cook when it starts to beep. After you hear a beep, open the top lid.
7. Arrange the steaks over the grill grate.
8. Close the top lid and cook for 4 minutes. Now open the top lid, flip the steaks.
9. Close the top lid and cook for 4 more minutes. Slice the steaks and serve warm.

Nutritional Values (Per Serving):
Calories: 351
Fat: 14g
Saturated Fat: 5g
Trans Fat: 0g
Carbohydrates: 8.5g
Fiber: 2g
Sodium: 954mg
Protein: 48g

Bourbon Pork Chops

Prep Time: 5-10 min.
Cooking Time: 20 min.
Number of Servings: 4
Ingredients:
4 boneless pork chops
Sea salt and ground black pepper to taste
¼ cup apple cider vinegar
¼ cup soy sauce
3 tablespoons Worcestershire sauce
2 cups ketchup
¾ cup bourbon
1 cup packed brown sugar
½ tablespoon dry mustard powder
Directions:
1. Take Ninja Foodi Grill, arrange it over your kitchen platform, and open the top lid. Arrange the grill grate and close the top lid.
2. Press "GRILL" and select the "MED" grill function. Adjust the timer to 15 minutes and then press "START/STOP." Ninja Foodi will start preheating.
3. Ninja Foodi is preheated and ready to cook when it starts to beep. After you hear a beep, open the top lid.
4. Arrange the pork chops over the grill grate.
5. Close the top lid and cook for 8 minutes. Now open the top lid, flip the pork chops.
6. Close the top lid and cook for 8 more minutes. Check the pork chops for doneness, cook for 2 more minutes if required.
7. In a saucepan, heat the soy sauce, sugar, ketchup, bourbon, vinegar, Worcestershire sauce, and mustard powder; stir-cook until boils.
8. Reduce heat and simmer for 20 minutes to thicken the sauce.
9. Season the pork chops with salt and black pepper. Serve warm with the prepared sauce.

Nutritional Values (Per Serving):
Calories: 346
Fat: 13.5g
Saturated Fat: 4g
Trans Fat: 0g
Carbohydrates: 27g
Fiber: 0.5g
Sodium: 1324mg
Protein: 27g

Shrimp Skewers with Yogurt Sauce

Prep Time: 5-10 min.
Cooking Time: 8 min.
Number of Servings: 4
Ingredients:
2/3 cup fresh arugula
1/3 cup lemon juice
1/4 cup yogurt
2 teaspoons milk
2 tablespoons olive oil
1 pound shrimp, peeled and deveined
2 green onions, sliced
1/2 teaspoon salt
1/4 teaspoon ground black pepper
1 teaspoon Dijon mustard
2 garlic cloves, minced
1/2 teaspoon grated lemon zest
1 teaspoon cider vinegar
1/2 teaspoon sugar
12 cherry tomatoes
Directions:
1. In a mixing bowl, season the shrimp with lemon juice, lemon zest, oil, and garlic. Set aside for 10-15 minutes.
2. Take food processor or blender, open the lid and inside add the arugula, yogurt, milk, green onion, sugar, vinegar, mustard, and ¼ teaspoon salt.
3. Blend to make a smooth mixture.
4. Take the skewers, thread the seasoned shrimp and tomatoes. Thread alternatively. Season the skewers with salt and black pepper.
5. Take Ninja Foodi Grill, arrange it over your kitchen platform, and open the top lid.
6. Arrange the grill grate and close the top lid.
7. Press "GRILL" and select the "MED" grill function. Adjust the timer to 4 minutes and then press "START/STOP." Ninja Foodi will start pre-heating.
8. Ninja Foodi is preheated and ready to cook when it starts to beep. After you hear a beep, open the top lid.
9. Arrange the skewers over the grill grate.
10. Close the top lid and cook for 2 minutes. Now open the top lid, flip the skewers.
11. Close the top lid and cook for 2 more minutes.
12. Serve with the prepared sauce.

Nutritional Values (Per Serving):

Calories: 334
Fat: 4g
Saturated Fat: 0.5g
Trans Fat: 0g
Carbohydrates: 28g
Fiber: 2.5g
Sodium: 547mg
Protein: 15.5g

Crisped Shrimp with Chili Sauce

Prep Time: 5-10 min.
Cooking Time: 15 min.
Number of Servings: 4
Ingredients:
2 large eggs
¼ cup panko bread crumbs
¾ cup coconut flakes, unsweetened
½ cup all-purpose flour
2 teaspoons ground black pepper
½ teaspoon sea salt
24 peeled, deveined shrimp
Chili sauce of your choice
Directions:
1. In a mixing bowl, add the flour, black pepper, and salt. Combine the ingredients to mix well with each other.
2. In another bowl, whisk the eggs. In another bowl, combine the coconut flakes and bread crumbs
3. Coat the shrimps with the flour mixture and then coat with the egg mixture. Lastly, coat with the coconut mixture.
4. Take Ninja Foodi Grill, arrange it over your kitchen platform, and open the top lid.
5. Arrange the Crisping Basket inside the pot. Coat it with some cooking spray.
6. Press "AIR CRISP" and adjust the temperature to 400°F. Adjust the timer to 7 minutes and then press "START/STOP." Ninja Foodi will start pre-heating.
7. Ninja Foodi is preheated and ready to cook when it starts to beep. After you hear a beep, open the top lid.
8. Arrange the shrimps directly inside the basket.
9. Close the top lid and allow it to cook until the timer reads zero. Cook in batches if needed.
10. Serve warm with chili sauce.

Nutritional Values (Per Serving):
Calories: 356
Fat: 13.5g
Saturated Fat: 8g
Trans Fat: 0g
Carbohydrates: 24.5g
Fiber: 4g
Sodium: 413mg
Protein: 31g

Fish Greens Bowl

Prep Time: 5-10 min.
Cooking Time: 6 min.
Number of Servings: 4
Ingredients:
6 tablespoons extra-virgin olive oil
1 ½ pounds tuna, cut into four strips
2 tablespoons rice wine vinegar
¼ teaspoon sea salt
½ teaspoon ground black pepper
2 tablespoons sesame oil
1 (10-ounce) bag baby greens
½ English cucumber, sliced
Directions:
1. In a mixing bowl, add the rice vinegar, ¼ teaspoon of salt, and ½ teaspoon of pepper. Combine the ingredients to mix well with each other.
2. Add the oil and combine again.
3. Season the fish with salt and pepper, and drizzle with the sesame oil.
4. Take Ninja Foodi Grill, arrange it over your kitchen platform, and open the top lid.
5. Arrange the grill grate and close the top lid.
6. Press "GRILL" and select the "MAX" grill function. Adjust the timer to 6 minutes and then press "START/STOP." Ninja Foodi will start pre-heating.
7. Ninja Foodi is preheated and ready to cook when it starts to beep. After you hear a beep, open the top lid.
8. Arrange the fish over the grill grate.
9. Close the top lid and allow to cook until the timer reads zero.
10. Serve warm with the baby greens, veggies, and vinaigrette on top.

Nutritional Values (Per Serving):

Calories: 418
Fat: 28g
Saturated Fat: 4.5g
Trans Fat: 0g
Carbohydrates: 6.5g
Fiber: 2g
Sodium: 208mg
Protein: 35g

BBQ Roasted Shrimps

Prep Time: 5-10 min.
Cooking Time: 7 min.
Number of Servings: 2
Ingredients:
3 tablespoons minced chipotles in adobo sauce
¼ teaspoon salt
1/4 cup barbecue sauce
Juice of 1/2 orange
½-pound large shrimps
Directions:
1. In a mixing bowl, add all the ingredients. Combine the ingredients to mix well with each other.
2. Set aside to marinate for 15 minutes.
3. Take Ninja Foodi Grill, arrange it over your kitchen platform, and open the top lid. Lightly grease cooking pot with some oil or cooking spray.
4. Press "ROAST" and adjust the temperature to 400°F. Adjust the timer to 7 minutes and then press "START/STOP." Ninja Foodi will start pre-heating.
5. Ninja Foodi is preheated and ready to cook when it starts to beep. After you hear a beep, open the top lid.
6. Arrange the shrimps directly inside the pot.
7. Close the top lid and allow it to cook until the timer reads zero.
8. Serve warm.

Nutritional Values (Per Serving):

Calories: 173
Fat: 2g
Saturated Fat: 0.5g
Trans Fat: 0g
Carbohydrates: 21g
Fiber: 2g
Sodium: 1143mg
Protein: 17.5g

Seafood Dinner Delight

Prep Time: 5-10 min.
Cooking Time: 19 min.
Number of Servings: 5-6

Ingredients:
1 pound sea bass fillets, cut into 2-inch chunks
1 ½ cups vegetable broth
2 pounds large shrimp, peeled and deveined
1 (28-ounce) can diced tomatoes, drained
¼ cup tomato paste
3 tablespoons Cajun seasoning
½ teaspoon sea salt
2 tablespoons extra-virgin olive oil
2 yellow onions, diced
2 bell peppers, diced
4 celery stalks, diced

Directions:
1. Season the fish evenly with 1 ½ tablespoon of Cajun seasoning and ¼ teaspoon of salt.
2. Take Ninja Foodi multi-cooker, arrange it over a cooking platform, and open the top lid.
3. In the pot, add 1 tablespoon oil; Select "SEAR/SAUTÉ" mode and select "MD: HI" pressure level.
4. Press "STOP/START." After about 4-5 minutes, the oil will start simmering.
5. Add the fish and cook (while stirring) until cooked well for about 4 minutes.
6. Set aside the fish.
7. In the pot, add the onions and remaining oil and cook (while stirring) until they become softened and translucent for 2-3 minutes.
8. Add the bell peppers, celery, and remaining Cajun seasoning; stir and cook for 2 minutes.
9. Add the fish, tomatoes, tomato paste, and broth; stir the mixture.
10. Seal the multi-cooker by locking it with the pressure lid; ensure to keep the pressure release valve locked/sealed.
11. Select "PRESSURE" mode and select the "HI" pressure level. Then, set timer to 5 minutes and press "STOP/START"; it will start the cooking process by building up inside pressure.
12. When the timer goes off, quick release pressure by adjusting the pressure valve to the VENT. After pressure gets released, open the pressure lid.
13. Select "SEAR/SAUTÉ" mode and select the "MD" pressure level; add the shrimps and combine them.

14. Seal the multi-cooker by locking it with the pressure lid; ensure to keep the pressure release valve locked/sealed.
15. Select "PRESSURE" mode and select the "HI" pressure level. Then, set timer to 4 minutes and press "STOP/START"; it will start the cooking process by building up inside pressure.
16. When the timer goes off, quick release pressure by adjusting the pressure valve to the VENT. After pressure gets released, open the pressure lid.
17. Take out the mixture and serve the cooked fish on top — season to taste with some salt.
18. Serve warm and enjoy!

Nutritional Values (Per Serving):
Calories:
Fat: g
Saturated Fat: g
Trans Fat: 0g
Carbohydrates: g
Fiber: g
Sodium: mg
Protein: g

Tuna Berry Meal

Prep Time: 5-10 min.
Cooking Time: 15 min.
Number of Servings: 4

Ingredients:
1 cup blackberries
½ teaspoon sweet paprika
1 tablespoon olive oil or vegetable oil
1 tablespoon balsamic vinegar
½ pound tuna, skinless, boneless and cut into small cubes
Black pepper and salt to the taste

Directions:
1. Take Ninja Foodi multi-cooker, arrange it over a cooking platform, and open the top lid.
2. In the pot, add the oil; Select "SEAR/SAUTÉ" mode and select "MD: HI" pressure level.
3. Press "STOP/START." After about 4-5 minutes, the oil will start simmering.
4. Add the berries, vinegar, paprika, black pepper, and salt; cook (while stirring) until it becomes softened and translucent for about 3 minutes.
5. Add the mixture in a blender and blend to prepare a smooth mixture.
6. Add the fish in the pot and top with the berry mixture.
7. Seal the multi-cooker by locking it with the pressure lid; ensure to keep the pressure release valve locked/sealed.
8. Select "PRESSURE" mode and select the "HI" pressure level. Then, set timer to 10 minutes and press "STOP/START"; it will start the cooking process by building up inside pressure.
9. When the timer goes off, quick release pressure by adjusting the pressure valve to the VENT. After pressure gets released, open the pressure lid.
10. Serve warm.

Nutritional Values (Per Serving):
Calories: 171
Fat: 6.5g
Saturated Fat: 1g
Trans Fat: 0g
Carbohydrates: 8g
Fiber: 2.5g
Sodium: 358mg
Protein: 15g

Couscous Fish Meal

Prep Time: 5-10 min.
Cooking Time: 20 min.
Number of Servings: 4

Ingredients:
Juice of 1 lemon
1 teaspoon grated lemon zest
1 teaspoon sea salt
4 (5- to 6-ounce) cod fillets
2 cups pearl couscous
2 ½ cups chicken broth
1 cup panko bread crumbs
1 tablespoon extra-virgin olive oil
1 red bell pepper, diced
1 yellow bell pepper, diced
½ stick butter, melted
¼ cup minced parsley

Directions:
1. In a mixing bowl, add the panko bread crumbs, butter, parsley, lemon juice, lemon zest, and salt. Combine the mixture well.
2. Add fish one by one and coat evenly with the crumb mixture.
3. Take Ninja Foodi multi-cooker, arrange it over a cooking platform, and open the top lid.
4. In the pot, add the oil; Select "SEAR/SAUTÉ" mode and select "MD: HI" pressure level.
5. Press "STOP/START." After about 4-5 minutes, the oil will start simmering.
6. Add the red and yellow bell peppers, and couscous; cook (while stirring) for about 1 minute.
7. Add the broth and combine it.
8. Seal the multi-cooker by locking it with the pressure lid; ensure to keep the pressure release valve locked/sealed.
9. Select "PRESSURE" mode and select the "HI" pressure level. Then, set timer to 6 minutes and press "STOP/START"; it will start the cooking process by building up inside pressure.
10. When the timer goes off, quick release pressure by adjusting the pressure valve to the VENT. After pressure gets released, open the pressure lid.
11. Over the couscous mixture, arrange the reversible rack. Arrange the fish fillets over it.
12. Seal the multi-cooker by locking it with the crisping lid; ensure to keep the pressure release valve locked/sealed.

13. Select the "AIR CRISP" mode and adjust the 350°F temperature level. Then, set timer to 12 minutes and press "STOP/START"; it will start the cooking process by building up inside pressure.
14. When the timer goes off, quick release pressure by adjusting the pressure valve to the VENT.
15. After pressure gets released, open the pressure lid. Check if the fish is cooked well; cook for 2 more minutes if needed.
16. Serve warm and enjoy!

Nutritional Values (Per Serving):
Calories: 658
Fat: 19.5g
Saturated Fat: 8g
Trans Fat: 0g
Carbohydrates: 63.5g
Fiber: 7g
Sodium: 951mg
Protein: 44.5g

Shrimp Pasta Mania

Prep Time: 5-10 min.
Cooking Time: 18 min.
Number of Servings: 4

Ingredients:
1 ¼ pounds medium raw shrimp, peeled and deveined
1 ½ teaspoons kosher salt
1 tablespoon extra-virgin olive oil
2 large garlic cloves, minced
½ teaspoon red pepper flakes
1 tablespoon lemon juice
1 teaspoon grated lemon zest
2 ½ cups water
⅓ cup tomato purée
¼ cup white wine
10 ounces farfalle or bow tie pasta
6 cups arugula leaves

Directions:
1. Take Ninja Foodi multi-cooker, arrange it over a cooking platform, and open the top lid.
2. In the pot, arrange a reversible rack and place the Crisping Basket over the rack.
3. In the basket, add the shrimps, ½ teaspoon of kosher salt, olive oil, and 1 minced garlic clove; stir gently to coat well.
4. Seal the multi-cooker by locking it with the crisping lid; ensure to keep the pressure release valve locked/sealed.
5. Select the "AIR CRISP" mode and adjust the 400°F temperature level. Then, set timer to 6 minutes and press "STOP/START"; it will start the cooking process by building up inside pressure.
6. When the timer goes off, quick release pressure by adjusting the pressure valve to the VENT.
7. After pressure gets released, open the pressure lid.
8. Remove the basket and set aside.
9. Select "SEAR/SAUTÉ" mode and select "HI" pressure level.
10. Press "STOP/START." After about 4-5 minutes, the oil will start simmering.
11. Add the wine and simmer the mixture for 1-2 minutes. Add the water, pasta and remaining salt, garlic clove, tomato purée, and red pepper flakes. Stir to combine.
12. Seal the multi-cooker by locking it with the pressure lid; ensure to keep the pressure release valve locked/sealed.

13. Select "PRESSURE" mode and select the "HI" pressure level. Then, set timer to 5 minutes and press "STOP/START"; it will start the cooking process by building up inside pressure.
14. When the timer goes off, quick release pressure by adjusting the pressure valve to the VENT. After pressure gets released, open the pressure lid.
15. Add the lemon juice and zest; stir and add the arugula and shrimp; combine and serve warm.

Nutritional Values (Per Serving):
Calories: 468
Fat: 8.5g
Saturated Fat: 1g
Trans Fat: 0g
Carbohydrates: 48.5g
Fiber: 3g
Sodium: 625mg
Protein: 38g

Shrimp & Mayonnaise Rice

Prep Time: 5-10 min.
Cooking Time: 10 min.
Number of Servings: 4

Ingredients:
16 ounces shrimps
½ cup mayonnaise
1 cup long-grain white rice
1 cup water
½ teaspoon Sriracha
¼ cup sweet chili sauce
2 tablespoons sliced scallions

Directions:
1. Take Ninja Foodi multi-cooker, arrange it over a cooking platform, and open the top lid.
2. In the pot, add the rice and water.
3. Seal the multi-cooker by locking it with the pressure lid; ensure to keep the pressure release valve locked/sealed.
4. Select "PRESSURE" mode and select the "HI" pressure level. Then, set timer to 2 minutes and press "STOP/START"; it will start the cooking process by building up inside pressure.
5. When the timer goes off, quick release pressure by adjusting the pressure valve to the VENT. After pressure gets released, open the pressure lid.
6. Over the rice, place the reversible rack; arrange the shrimps over.
7. Seal the multi-cooker by locking it with the crisping lid; ensure to keep the pressure release valve locked/sealed.
8. Select the "AIR CRISP" mode and adjust the 390°F temperature level. Then, set timer to 10 minutes and press "STOP/START"; it will start the cooking process by building up inside pressure.
9. When the timer goes off, quick release pressure by adjusting the pressure valve to the VENT.
10. After pressure gets released, open the pressure lid.
11. Take a mixing bowl, add the mayonnaise, sweet chili sauce, and Sriracha; combine well.
12. Add the shrimps and combine them well. Serve the shrimps with cooked rice and scallions on top.

Nutritional Values (Per Serving):

Calories: 413

Fat: 11g

Saturated Fat: 2g

Trans Fat: 0g

Carbohydrates: 46.5g

Fiber: 2g

Sodium: 628mg

Protein: 26g

Classic Cream & Shrimp

Prep Time: 5-10 min.
Cooking Time: 10 min.
Number of Servings: 2-4

Ingredients:
1 pound shrimp, peeled and deveined
2 garlic cloves, minced
1 tablespoons butter, melted
½ cup chicken stock
¼ cup heavy cream
1 tablespoons chives, chopped
1 tablespoons parsley, chopped
Lemon wedges to serve
Black pepper and salt to the taste

Directions:
1. Take Ninja Foodi multi-cooker, arrange it over a cooking platform, and open the top lid.
2. In the pot, add the butter; Select "SEAR/SAUTÉ" mode and select "MD: HI" pressure level.
3. Press "STOP/START." After about 4-5 minutes, the butter will start simmering.
4. Add the garlic, chives, and cook (while stirring) for about 2 minutes.
5. Add the shrimp, cream, salt, pepper, stock, and parsley; combine well.
6. Seal the multi-cooker by locking it with the pressure lid; ensure to keep the pressure release valve locked/sealed.
7. Select "PRESSURE" mode and select the "HI" pressure level. Then, set timer to 8 minutes and press "STOP/START"; it will start the cooking process by building up inside pressure.
8. When the timer goes off, quick release pressure by adjusting the pressure valve to the VENT. After pressure gets released, open the pressure lid.
9. Serve warm with some lemon wedges and enjoy!

Nutritional Values (Per Serving):
Calories: 426
Fat: 27g
Saturated Fat: 8g
Trans Fat: 0g
Carbohydrates: 13g
Fiber: 3g
Sodium: 856mg
Protein: 38.5g

Potato Fish Baked Meal

Prep Time: 10 min.
Cooking Time: 25 min.
Number of Servings: 4

Ingredients:
1 ½ cups heavy cream
1 pound gold potatoes, cut into small cubes
1 yellow onion, chopped
4 sea bass fillets, boneless
Cooking spray
Ground black pepper and salt to the taste

Directions:
1. Take a baking pan; grease it with some cooking spray, vegetable oil, or butter. In the pan, mix all the ingredients except the fish.
2. Take Ninja Foodi multi-cooker, arrange it over a cooking platform, and open the top lid.
3. In the pot, add water and place a reversible rack inside the pot. Place the pan over the rack. Place the fish in the pan on top.
4. Seal the multi-cooker by locking it with the crisping lid; ensure to keep the pressure release valve locked/sealed.
5. Select "BAKE/ROAST" mode and adjust the 380°F temperature level. Then, set timer to 25 minutes and press "STOP/START"; it will start the cooking process by building up inside pressure.
6. When the timer goes off, quick release pressure by adjusting the pressure valve to the VENT. After pressure gets released, open the pressure lid.
7. Serve warm and enjoy!

Nutritional Values (Per Serving):
Calories: 523
Fat: 23.5g
Saturated Fat: 11g
Trans Fat: 0g
Carbohydrates: 30.5g
Fiber: 6g
Sodium: 429mg
Protein: 39g

Broccoli Salmon Rice Meal

Prep Time: 5-10 min.
Cooking Time: 10 min.
Number of Servings: 4

Ingredients:
1 small head broccoli, cut into florets
3 tablespoons extra-virgin olive oil
1 cup brown rice, rinsed
¾ cup water
4 (4-ounce) frozen skinless salmon fillets
1 teaspoon black pepper, freshly ground
1 teaspoon sea salt
Juice of 2 limes
1 teaspoon paprika
4 garlic cloves, minced
2 jalapeño peppers, seeded and diced
2 tablespoons fresh parsley, chopped
2 tablespoons honey

Directions:
1. Take Ninja Foodi multi-cooker, arrange it over a cooking platform, and open the top lid.
2. In the pot, add water, rice, and place a reversible rack inside the pot. Place the salmon fillets over the rack.
3. Seal the multi-cooker by locking it with the pressure lid; ensure to keep the pressure release valve locked/sealed.
4. Select "PRESSURE" mode and select the "HI" pressure level. Then, set timer to 2 minutes and press "STOP/START"; it will start the cooking process by building up inside pressure.
5. When the timer goes off, quick release pressure by adjusting the pressure valve to the VENT. After pressure gets released, open the pressure lid.
6. Take out the salmon and reserve the cooked rice.
7. In a mixing bowl, add the broccoli, one tablespoon olive oil, salt, and black pepper. Toss well.
8. In another bowl, add the remaining two tablespoons oil, lime juice, honey, paprika, garlic, jalapeño, and parsley. Combine well. Add the cooked fillets in the bowl and combine.
9. Add the mixture in the pot and add the broccoli mixture on top.
10. Seal the multi-cooker by locking it with the crisping lid; ensure to keep the pressure release valve locked/sealed.
11. Select "BROIL" mode and select the "HI" pressure level. Then, set timer to 7 minutes and press "STOP/START"; it will start the cooking process by building up inside pressure.
12. When the timer goes off, quick release pressure by adjusting the pressure valve to the VENT.
13. After pressure gets released, open the pressure lid.
14. Serve the salmon warm with rice and some parsley on top and enjoy!

Nutritional Values (Per Serving):

Calories: 456
Fat: 18g
Saturated Fat: 3g
Trans Fat: 0g
Carbohydrates: 46g
Fiber: 5.5g
Sodium: 628mg
Protein: 27g

Herbed Codfish Meal

Prep Time: 10 min.
Cooking Time: 8 min.
Number of Servings: 5-6

Ingredients:
6 medium eggs
2 small onions, chopped finely
4 garlic cloves, minced
2 teaspoons soy sauce
¼ cup butter, melted
2 green chilies, chopped finely
3 (4-ounce) skinless codfish fillets, cut into rectangle shape pieces
Ground black pepper and salt to taste

Directions:
1. Take a mixing bowl and add all ingredients in it except fish. Combine well, add the fish pieces and combine well.
2. In the Crisping basket, add the mixture.
3. Take Ninja Foodi multi-cooker, arrange it over a cooking platform, and open the top lid.
4. In the pot, add water and place a reversible rack inside the pot. Place the Crisping basket over the rack.
5. Seal the multi-cooker by locking it with the crisping lid; ensure to keep the pressure release valve locked/sealed.
6. Select the "AIR CRISP" mode and adjust the 330°F temperature level. Then, set timer to 8 minutes and press "STOP/START"; it will start the cooking process by building up inside pressure.
7. When the timer goes off, quick release pressure by adjusting the pressure valve to the VENT.
8. After pressure gets released, open the pressure lid.
9. Serve warm and enjoy!

Nutritional Values (Per Serving):
Calories: 416
Fat: 23.5g
Saturated Fat: 11g
Trans Fat: 0g
Carbohydrates: 9g
Fiber: 1g
Sodium: 401mg
Protein: 36g

Prep Time: 5-10 min.
Cooking Time: 2 min.
Number of Servings: 4

Ingredients:
4 chorizo sausages, sliced
1 pound shrimp, peeled and deveined
1 lemon, cut into wedges
3 red potatoes
¼ cup butter, melted
3 ears corn, cut into 1 ½-inch rounds
2 cups water
1 cup white wine
2 tablespoon seasoning mix of your choice
Salt to taste

Directions:
1. Take Ninja Foodi multi-cooker, arrange it over a cooking platform, and open the top lid.
2. In the pot, add all ingredients except butter and lemon wedges. Do not stir.
3. Seal the multi-cooker by locking it with the pressure lid; ensure to keep the pressure release valve locked/sealed.
4. Select "PRESSURE" mode and select the "HI" pressure level. Then, set timer to 2 minutes and press "STOP/START"; it will start the cooking process by building up inside pressure.
5. When the timer goes off, quick release pressure by adjusting the pressure valve to the VENT. After pressure gets released, open the pressure lid.
6. Drain excess liquid by passing the mixture through a colander. Add in serving plates, top with the melted butter.
7. Serve warm with some lemon wedges and enjoy!

Nutritional Values (Per Serving):
Calories: 742
Fat: 30g
Saturated Fat: 12.5g
Trans Fat: 0g
Carbohydrates: 39g
Fiber: 9g
Sodium: 712mg
Protein: 33g

Ginger Garlic Salmon

Prep Time: 5-10 min.
Cooking Time: 30 min.
Number of Servings: 3-4

Ingredients:
3 green chilies, chopped
1 pound salmon fillets
2 tablespoons ginger-garlic paste
Ground black pepper and salt to taste
¾ cup butter, melted

Directions:
1. Season the salmon with salt, pepper, and ginger paste.
2. Take a baking pan; grease it with some cooking spray, vegetable oil, or butter. Add the salmon mixture and add the chilies and butter on top.
3. Take Ninja Foodi multi-cooker, arrange it over a cooking platform, and open the top lid.
4. In the pot, add water and place a reversible rack inside the pot. Place the pan over the rack.
5. Seal the multi-cooker by locking it with the crisping lid; ensure to keep the pressure release valve locked/sealed.
6. Select "BAKE/ROAST" mode and adjust the 360°F temperature level. Then, set timer to 30 minutes and press "STOP/START"; it will start the cooking process by building up inside pressure.
7. When the timer goes off, quick release pressure by adjusting the pressure valve to the VENT. After pressure gets released, open the pressure lid.
8. Serve warm and enjoy!

Nutritional Values (Per Serving):
Calories: 486
Fat: 38g
Saturated Fat: 16g
Trans Fat: 0g
Carbohydrates: 7g
Fiber: 2g
Sodium: 314mg
Protein: 22.5g

Wholesome Salmon Spinach

Prep Time: 5-10 min.
Cooking Time: 10 min.
Number of Servings: 4

Ingredients:
½ cup chicken stock
1 tablespoon olive oil or vegetable oil
2 cups baby spinach
2 salmon fillets, boneless and cut into cubes
A pinch of ground black pepper and salt
1 tablespoon parsley, chopped

Directions:
1. Take Ninja Foodi multi-cooker, arrange it over a cooking platform, and open the top lid.
2. In the pot, add the oil; Select "SEAR/SAUTÉ" mode and select "MD: HI" pressure level.
3. Press "STOP/START." After about 4-5 minutes, the oil will start simmering.
4. Add the salmon and cook (while stirring) to soften and sear for 1 minute on each side.
5. Add other ingredients except for the parsley; stir the mixture.
6. Seal the multi-cooker by locking it with the pressure lid; ensure to keep the pressure release valve locked/sealed.
7. Select "PRESSURE" mode and select the "HI" pressure level. Then, set timer to 10 minutes and press "STOP/START"; it will start the cooking process by building up inside pressure.
8. When the timer goes off, naturally release inside pressure for about 8-10 minutes. Then, quick-release pressure by adjusting the pressure valve to the VENT.
9. After pressure gets released, open the pressure lid.
10. Serve warm with some chopped parsley on top and enjoy!

Nutritional Values (Per Serving):
Calories: 203
Fat: 7g
Saturated Fat: 1g
Trans Fat: 0g
Carbohydrates: 6.5g
Fiber: 2g
Sodium: 312mg
Protein: 18g

Tilapia & Green Cabbage

Prep Time: 5-10 min.
Cooking Time: 25 min.
Number of Servings: 4

Ingredients:
1 cup green cabbage, shredded
½ teaspoon chili powder
2 tablespoons avocado oil or vegetable oil
4 tilapia fillets, boneless
2 tablespoons parsley, chopped
Ground black pepper and salt to the taste

Directions:
1. Take a baking pan; grease it with some cooking spray, vegetable oil, or butter. Add the fish and other ingredients. Combine well.
2. Take Ninja Foodi multi-cooker, arrange it over a cooking platform, and open the top lid.
3. In the pot, add water and place a reversible rack inside the pot. Place the - over the rack.
4. Seal the multi-cooker by locking it with the crisping lid; ensure to keep the pressure release valve locked/sealed.
5. Select "BAKE/ROAST" mode and adjust the 380°F temperature level. Then, set timer to 25 minutes and press "STOP/START"; it will start the cooking process by building up inside pressure.
6. When the timer goes off, quick release pressure by adjusting the pressure valve to the VENT. After pressure gets released, open the pressure lid.
7. Serve warm and enjoy!

Nutritional Values (Per Serving):
Calories: 143
Fat: 4g
Saturated Fat: 0.5g
Trans Fat: 0g
Carbohydrates: 7.5g
Fiber: 2g
Sodium: 234mg
Protein: 22g

Spinach Fish Curry

Prep Time: 5-10 min.
Cooking Time: 5 min.
Number of Servings: 4

Ingredients:
1 tablespoon Thai red curry paste
½ cup water
1 (14-ounce) can coconut milk
Vegetable oil to cook
1 small onion, sliced
1 medium zucchini, cut into thick rounds
1 pound frozen cod or grouper fillets
1 teaspoon lime juice (optional)
1 small seeded red bell pepper, cut into bite-size pieces
1 small (5-ounce) bag baby spinach
1 cup cherry tomatoes, halved
2 tablespoons chopped basil
¼ cup roasted salted cashews, coarsely chopped

Directions:
1. ake Ninja Foodi multi-cooker, arrange it over a cooking platform, and open the top lid.
2. In the pot, add the oil; Select "SEAR/SAUTÉ" mode and select "MD: HI" pressure level.
3. Press "STOP/START." After about 4-5 minutes, the oil will start simmering.
4. Add the curry paste and cook (while stirring) to mix with the oil. Add the coconut milk and stir.
5. Add the water, zucchini, onion, bell pepper, and fish fillets; stir the mixture.
6. Seal the multi-cooker by locking it with the pressure lid; ensure to keep the pressure release valve locked/sealed.
7. Select "PRESSURE" mode and select the "LO" pressure level. Then, set timer to 3 minutes and press "STOP/START"; it will start the cooking process by building up inside pressure.
8. When the timer goes off, quick release pressure by adjusting the pressure valve to the VENT. After pressure gets released, open the pressure lid.
9. Make small pieces from the cooked fish.
10. Select "SEAR/SAUTÉ" mode and select the "MD" pressure level; add the tomatoes, lime juice, and spinach; combine. Stir-cook until heated through.
11. Serve warm with basil and cashews on top, and enjoy!

Nutritional Values (Per Serving):

Calories: 386
Fat: 24.5g
Saturated Fat: 16g
Trans Fat: 0g
Carbohydrates: 17g
Fiber: 4g
Sodium: 187mg
Protein: 25g

Broccoli Pasta Mania

Prep Time: 5-10 min.
Cooking Time: 15 min.
Number of Servings: 4

Ingredients:
3 tablespoons olive oil
3 teaspoons kosher salt
10 ounces fettucine pasta, broken in half
1 bunch asparagus, trimmed, cut into 1-inch pieces
2 cups small broccoli florets
3 garlic cloves, minced
2 ½ cups water
½ cup grated Parmesan cheese
¼ cup chopped parsley or basil
½ cup heavy whipping cream
1 cup cherry tomatoes, halved

Directions:
1. Take Ninja Foodi multi-cooker, arrange it over a cooking platform, and open the top lid.
2. In the pot, arrange a reversible rack and place the Crisping Basket over the rack.
3. In the basket, add the asparagus and broccoli. Add 1 tablespoon olive oil and ½ teaspoon of kosher salt; stir the mixture.
4. Seal the multi-cooker by locking it with the crisping lid; ensure to keep the pressure release valve locked/sealed.
5. Select the "AIR CRISP" mode and adjust the 375°F temperature level. Then, set timer to 2 minutes and press "STOP/START"; it will start the cooking process by building up inside pressure.
6. When the timer goes off, quick release pressure by adjusting the pressure valve to the VENT.
7. After pressure gets released, open the pressure lid. Set aside the basket.
8. In the pot, add the pasta and remaining oil. Stir to coat evenly.
9. Add remaining kosher salt, garlic, and water.
10. Seal the multi-cooker by locking it with the pressure lid; ensure to keep the pressure release valve locked/sealed.
11. Select "PRESSURE" mode and select the "HI" pressure level. Then, set timer to 5 minutes and press "STOP/START"; it will start the cooking process by building up inside pressure.

12. When the timer goes off, quick release pressure by adjusting the pressure valve to VENT. After pressure gets released, open the pressure lid.
13. Select "SEAR/SAUTÉ" mode and select the "MD" pressure level; add the heavy cream and tomatoes. Stir-cook until the sauce thickens.
14. Add the broccoli and asparagus; serve with some herbs and cheese on top.

Nutritional Values (Per Serving):
Calories: 524
Fat: 24.5g
Saturated Fat: 10.5g
Trans Fat: 0g
Carbohydrates: 51.5g
Fiber: 5g
Sodium: 626mg
Protein: 17.5g

Spiced Chickpeas Rice

Prep Time: 5-10 min.
Cooking Time: 18 min.
Number of Servings: 6-8

Ingredients:
6 garlic cloves, minced
28 ounce canned tomatoes, chopped
14 ounce coconut milk
1 pound chickpeas
1 yellow onion, chopped
A pinch of black pepper and salt
1 bunch cilantro, chopped
4 tablespoons coconut oil
1 tablespoons grated ginger
1 green chili pepper, chopped
2 ½ cups water
2 teaspoon garam masala or spice mix
2 teaspoon sugar
1 teaspoon chili powder
1 teaspoon turmeric powder
1 tablespoons cumin, ground
Juice of 2 lemons
Cooked rice to serve

Directions:
1. Take Ninja Foodi multi-cooker, arrange it over a cooking platform, and open the top lid.
2. In the pot, add the oil; Select "SEAR/SAUTÉ" mode and select "MD: HI" pressure level.
3. Press "STOP/START." After about 4-5 minutes, the oil will start simmering.
4. Add the onions, cumin, black pepper, and salt; cook (while stirring) until it becomes softened and translucent for about 4 minutes.
5. Add the turmeric, garlic, ginger, chili, chili powder, and cilantro, stir-cook for 2 minutes.
6. Add the tomatoes, water, coconut milk and chickpeas; combine again.
7. Seal the multi-cooker by locking it with the pressure lid; ensure to keep the pressure release valve locked/sealed.
8. Select "PRESSURE" mode and select the "LO" pressure level. Then, set timer to 10 minutes and press "STOP/START"; it will start the cooking process by building up inside pressure.
9. When the timer goes off, naturally release inside pressure for about 8-10 minutes. Then, quick-release pressure by adjusting the pressure valve to VENT.

10. Select "SEAR/SAUTÉ" mode and select the "MD" pressure level; add the sugar, garam masala, and lemon juice. Stir-cook for 4 minutes.
11. Serve warm with cooked rice.

Nutritional Values (Per Serving):
Calories: 201
Fat: 11.5g
Saturated Fat: 1g
Trans Fat: 0g
Carbohydrates: 21g
Fiber: 4g
Sodium: 589mg
Protein: 13.5g

Classic Leek Potato Soup

Prep Time: 5-10 min.
Cooking Time: 15 min.
Number of Servings: 5-6
Ingredients:

4 garlic cloves, minced
5 Yukon Gold potatoes, peeled
2 tablespoons extra-virgin olive oil
4 leeks, cleaned and thinly sliced
5 cups vegetable broth
¾ cup white wine
1 ½ cups light cream
½ cup grated Cheddar cheese
3 thyme sprigs, stems removed
2 bay leaves
½ teaspoon ground black pepper
1 ½ teaspoons dried oregano
1 teaspoon sea salt

Directions:
1. Take Ninja Foodi multi-cooker, arrange it over a cooking platform, and open the top lid.
2. In the pot, add the oil; Select "SEAR/SAUTÉ" mode and select "MD: HI" pressure level.
3. Press "STOP/START." After about 4-5 minutes, the oil will start simmering.
4. Add 3/4ᵗʰ leeks and cook (while stirring) until turn softened for 4-5 minutes.
5. Add the garlic and cook for 1 minute.
6. Add the potatoes, thyme, bay leaves, vegetable broth, white wine, oregano, salt, and black pepper; combine well.
7. Seal the multi-cooker by locking it with the pressure lid; ensure to keep the pressure release valve locked/sealed.
8. Select "PRESSURE" mode and select the "HI" pressure level. Then, set timer to 10 minutes and press "STOP/START"; it will start the cooking process by building up inside pressure.
9. When the timer goes off, quick release pressure by adjusting the pressure valve to VENT. After pressure gets released, open the pressure lid.
10. Take out the bay leaves; add the cream and mash to make a smooth mixture. Add the cheese on top.
11. In a mixing bowl, add the remaining leeks and remaining oil.
12. In the pot, add the reversible rack and place the leeks on top.
13. Seal the multi-cooker by locking it with the crisping lid; ensure to keep the pressure release valve locked/sealed.

14. Select "BROIL" mode and select the "HI" pressure level. Then, set timer to 5 minutes and press "STOP/START"; it will start the cooking process by building up inside pressure.
15. When the timer goes off, quick release pressure by adjusting the pressure valve to VENT.
16. After pressure gets released, open the pressure lid.
17. Serve the soup with the leeks on top.

Nutritional Values (Per Serving):
Calories: 372
Fat: 19g
Saturated Fat: 8g
Trans Fat: 0g
Carbohydrates: 48g
Fiber: 3.5g
Sodium: 852mg
Protein: 9g

Brown Rice Tofu Meal

Prep Time: 5-10 min.
Cooking Time: 30 min.
Number of Servings: 4

Ingredients:
1 sweet potato, peeled and diced
2 tablespoons extra-virgin olive oil
1 cup brown rice, rinsed
¾ cup water
1 teaspoon black pepper, freshly ground
1 teaspoon sea salt
1 (15-ounce) block extra-firm tofu, drained and cut into small cubes
2 teaspoons cornstarch
1 tablespoon soy sauce

Directions:
1. In a mixing bowl, add the sweet potato, salt, black pepper, and coat with one tablespoon of olive oil.
2. In another mixing bowl, add remaining olive oil and soy sauce. Add the tofu and toss well. Add the cornstarch and stir until evenly coated.
3. Take Ninja Foodi multi-cooker, arrange it over a cooking platform, and open the top lid.
4. In the pot, add the water and rice.
5. Seal the multi-cooker by locking it with the pressure lid; ensure to keep the pressure release valve locked/sealed.
6. Select "PRESSURE" mode and select the "HI" pressure level. Then, set timer to 2 minutes and press "STOP/START"; it will start the cooking process by building up inside pressure.
7. When the timer goes off, quick release pressure by adjusting the pressure valve to the VENT. After pressure gets released, open the pressure lid.
8. In the pot, place a reversible rack inside the pot. Place the sweet potatoes and tofu over the rack.
9. Seal the multi-cooker by locking it with the crisping lid; ensure to keep the pressure release valve locked/sealed.
10. Select the "AIR CRISP" mode and adjust the 400°F temperature level. Then, set timer to 20 minutes and press "STOP/START"; it will start the cooking process by building up inside pressure.
11. When the timer goes off, quick release pressure by adjusting the pressure valve to the VENT.
12. After pressure gets released, open the pressure lid.
13. Serve warm with the cooked rice and enjoy!

Nutritional Values (Per Serving):

Calories: 316
Fat: 10g
Saturated Fat: 2.5g
Trans Fat: 0g
Carbohydrates: 41g
Fiber: 4g
Sodium: 924mg
Protein: 12g

Prep Time: 5-10 min.
Cooking Time: 10 min.
Number of Servings: 4

Ingredients:
1 head broccoli, cut into florets
4 cups vegetable broth
2 ½ pounds potatoes, peeled and chopped
½ cup heavy cream
⅓ cup butter, melted
1 onion, chopped
2 cloves garlic, minced
½ cup chopped scallions
Ground black pepper and salt to taste
Cheddar cheese to serve

Directions:
1. Take Ninja Foodi multi-cooker, arrange it over a cooking platform, and open the top lid.
2. In the pot, add the butter; Select "SEAR/SAUTÉ" mode and select "MD: HI" pressure level.
3. Press "STOP/START." After about 4-5 minutes, the butter will start simmering.
4. Add the onions, garlic, and cook (while stirring) for 3-4 minutes until they become softened and translucent.
5. Add the broth, potatoes, and broccoli and mix well.
6. Seal the multi-cooker by locking it with the pressure lid; ensure to keep the pressure release valve locked/sealed.
7. Select "PRESSURE" mode and select the "HI" pressure level. Then, set timer to 5 minutes and press "STOP/START"; it will start the cooking process by building up inside pressure.
8. When the timer goes off, quick release pressure by adjusting the pressure valve to the VENT. After pressure gets released, open the pressure lid.
9. Add the potato mixture in a blender and blend well to puree the mixture. Add the heavy cream and season with pepper and salt to taste; combine well.
10. Serve with scallions and cheese on top.

Nutritional Values (Per Serving):
Calories: 549
Fat: 27.5g
Saturated Fat: 8g
Trans Fat: 0g
Carbohydrates: 36g
Fiber: 9.5g
Sodium: 547mg
Protein: 19g

Spinach Olive Meal

Prep Time: 5-10 min.
Cooking Time: 15 min.
Number of Servings: 5-6

Ingredients:
2/3 cup Kalamata olives, halved and pitted
1 ½ cups feta cheese, grated
4 tablespoons butter
2 pounds spinach, chopped and boiled
Ground black pepper and salt to taste
4 teaspoons grated lemon zest

Directions:
1. In a mixing bowl, add the spinach, butter, salt, pepper.
2. Take Ninja Foodi multi-cooker, arrange it over a cooking platform, and open the top lid.
3. In the pot, arrange a reversible rack and place the Crisping Basket over the rack.
4. In the basket, add the spinach mixture.
5. Seal the multi-cooker by locking it with the crisping lid; ensure to keep the pressure release valve locked/sealed.
6. Select the "AIR CRISP" mode and adjust the 340°F temperature level. Then, set timer to 15 minutes and press "STOP/START"; it will start the cooking process by building up inside pressure.
7. When the timer goes off, quick release pressure by adjusting the pressure valve to the VENT.
8. After pressure gets released, open the pressure lid.
9. Serve warm and enjoy!

Nutritional Values (Per Serving):
Calories: 253
Fat: 18g
Saturated Fat: 3g
Trans Fat: 0g
Carbohydrates: 8g
Fiber: 4g
Sodium: 339mg
Protein: 10.5g

Spinach Chickpea Stew

Prep Time: 5-10 min.
Cooking Time: 5 min.
Number of Servings: 5-6

Ingredients:
4 sweet potatoes, peeled and diced
4 cups vegetable broth
1 tablespoon extra-virgin olive oil
1 yellow onion, diced
4 garlic cloves, minced
4 cups baby spinach
2 (15-ounce) cans chickpeas, drained
1 (15-ounce) can fire-roasted diced tomatoes, undrained
1 teaspoon ground coriander
½ teaspoon black pepper, freshly ground
½ teaspoon paprika
½ teaspoon sea salt
1 ½ teaspoons ground cumin

Directions:
1. Take Ninja Foodi multi-cooker, arrange it over a cooking platform, and open the top lid.
2. In the pot, add the oil; Select "SEAR/SAUTÉ" mode and select "MD: HI" pressure level.
3. Press "STOP/START." After about 4-5 minutes, the oil will start simmering.
4. Add the onions, garlic, and cook (while stirring) until they become softened and translucent.
5. Add the sweet potatoes, broth, tomatoes, chickpeas, cumin, coriander, paprika, salt, and black pepper; stir the mixture.
6. Seal the multi-cooker by locking it with the pressure lid; ensure to keep the pressure release valve locked/sealed.
7. Select "PRESSURE" mode and select the "HI" pressure level. Then, set timer to 8 minutes and press "STOP/START"; it will start the cooking process by building up inside pressure.
8. When the timer goes off, quick release pressure by adjusting the pressure valve to the VENT. After pressure gets released, open the pressure lid.
9. Select "SEAR/SAUTÉ" mode and select the "MD" pressure level; add the spinach and combine. Stir-cook until wilts.
10. Serve warm and enjoy!

Nutritional Values (Per Serving):

Calories: 234
Fat: 4.5g
Saturated Fat: 0g
Trans Fat: 0g
Carbohydrates: 39.5g
Fiber: 9g
Sodium: 576mg
Protein: 8g

Prep Time: 10 min.
Cooking Time: 15 min.
Number of Servings: 4

Ingredients:
1 ½ cups panko bread crumbs
⅓ cup Parmesan cheese, grated
1 large eggplant, cut into thick rounds
2 teaspoons kosher salt
2 cups Marinara Sauce
1 cup shredded mozzarella cheese
3 tablespoons unsalted butter, melted

Directions:
1. Season the eggplant slices with the salt; allow to drain for 10 minutes. Shake off the liquid and dry out.
2. In a mixing bowl, combine the butter, panko, and Parmesan cheese. Set aside.
3. Take Ninja Foodi multi-cooker, arrange it over a cooking platform, and open the top lid.
4. In the pot, add the eggplant slices and marinara sauce.
5. Seal the multi-cooker by locking it with the pressure lid; ensure to keep the pressure release valve locked/sealed.
6. Select "PRESSURE" mode and select the "HI" pressure level. Then, set timer to 5 minutes and press "STOP/START"; it will start the cooking process by building up inside pressure.
7. When the timer goes off, quick release pressure by adjusting the pressure valve to the VENT. After pressure gets released, open the pressure lid.
8. Add the mozzarella cheese on top.
9. Seal the multi-cooker by locking it with the crisping lid; ensure to keep the pressure release valve locked/sealed.
10. Select "BAKE/ROAST" mode and adjust the 375°F temperature level. Then, set timer to 2 minutes and press "STOP/START"; it will start the cooking process by building up inside pressure.
11. When the timer goes off, quick release pressure by adjusting the pressure valve to the VENT. After pressure gets released, open the pressure lid.
12. Add the panko mixture on top.
13. Seal the multi-cooker by locking it with the crisping lid; ensure to keep the pressure release valve locked/sealed.
14. Select "BAKE/ROAST" mode and adjust the 375°F temperature level. Then, set timer to 8 minutes and press "STOP/START"; it will start the cooking process by building up inside pressure.
15. When the timer goes off, quick release pressure by adjusting the pressure valve to the VENT. After pressure gets released, open the pressure lid.
16. Serve warm and enjoy!

Nutritional Values (Per Serving):

Calories: 431
Fat: 19g
Saturated Fat: 9g
Trans Fat: 0g
Carbohydrates: 46g
Fiber: 9.5g
Sodium: 928mg
Protein: 19g

Broccoli Cheese Salad

Prep Time: 5-10 min.
Cooking Time: 12 min.
Number of Servings: 4
Ingredients:
1 tablespoon canola oil
1 teaspoon honey
1 teaspoon Dijon mustard
2 tablespoons extra-virgin olive oil
1 tablespoon lemon juice
2 heads broccoli, trimmed into florets
½ red onion, sliced
1 garlic clove, minced
Pinch red pepper flakes
Freshly ground black pepper
¼ teaspoon fine sea salt
4 cups arugula, chopped
2 tablespoons Parmesan cheese, grated

Directions:
1. In a mixing bowl, add the broccoli, sliced onions, and oil. Combine well.
2. In a mixing bowl, whisk the olive oil, lemon juice, honey, mustard, garlic, red pepper flakes, salt, and black pepper. Combine well.
3. Take Ninja Foodi Grill, arrange it over your kitchen platform, and open the top lid.
4. Arrange the grill grate and close the top lid.
5. Press "GRILL" and select the "MAX" grill function. Adjust the timer to 12 minutes and then press "START/STOP." Ninja Foodi will start preheating.
6. Ninja Foodi is preheated and ready to cook when it starts to beep. After you hear a beep, open the top lid.
7. Arrange the vegetables over the grill grate.
8. Close the top lid and allow it to cook until the timer reads zero.
9. Combine the broccoli mixture with the arugula and serve with the prepared vinaigrette and cheese on top.

Nutritional Values (Per Serving):
Calories: 179
Fat: 12g
Saturated Fat: 2.5g
Trans Fat: 0g
Carbohydrates: 15.5g
Fiber: 4g
Sodium: 253mg
Protein: 6.5g

Mushroom Tomato Roast

Prep Time: 10 min.
Cooking Time: 15 min.
Number of Servings: 4
Ingredients:
2 cups cherry tomatoes
2 cups cremini, button, or other small mushrooms
1/4 cup red wine or Sherry vinegar
2 garlic cloves, finely chopped
1/2 cup extra-virgin olive oil
3 tablespoons chopped thyme
Pinch of crushed red pepper flakes
1 teaspoon kosher salt
1/2 teaspoon black pepper
6 scallions, cut crosswise into 2-inch pieces
Directions:

1. Take a zip-lock bag, add black pepper, salt, red pepper flakes, thyme, vinegar, oil, and garlic. Add mushrooms, tomatoes, and scallions.
2. Shake well and refrigerate for 30-40 minutes to marinate.
3. Take Ninja Foodi Grill, arrange it over your kitchen platform, and open the top lid.
4. Press "BAKE" and adjust the temperature to 400°F. Adjust the timer to 12 minutes and then press "START/STOP." Ninja Foodi will start preheating.
5. Ninja Foodi is preheated and ready to cook when it starts to beep. After you hear a beep, open the top lid.
6. Arrange the mushroom mixture directly inside the pot.
7. Close the top lid and allow it to cook until the timer reads zero.
8. Serve warm.

Nutritional Values (Per Serving):
Calories: 253
Fat: 24g
Saturated Fat: 4g
Trans Fat: 0g
Carbohydrates: 7g
Fiber: 2g
Sodium: 546mg
Protein: 1g

Cheddar Cauliflower Meal

Prep Time: 5-10 min.
Cooking Time: 15 min.
Number of Servings: 2
Ingredients:
½ teaspoon garlic powder
½ teaspoon paprika
Sea salt and ground black pepper to taste
1 head cauliflower, stemmed and leaves removed
1 cup Cheddar cheese, shredded
Ranch dressing, for garnish
¼ cup canola oil or vegetable oil
2 tablespoons chopped chives
4 slices bacon, cooked and crumbled

Directions:
1. Cut the cauliflower into 2-inch pieces.
2. In a mixing bowl, add the oil, garlic powder, and paprika. Season with salt and ground black pepper; combine well. Coat the florets with the mixture.
3. Take Ninja Foodi Grill, arrange it over your kitchen platform, and open the top lid.
4. Arrange the grill grate and close the top lid.
5. Press "GRILL" and select the "MAX" grill function. Adjust the timer to 15 minutes and then press "START/STOP." Ninja Foodi will start preheating.
6. Ninja Foodi is preheated and ready to cook when it starts to beep. After you hear a beep, open the top lid.
7. Arrange the pieces over the grill grate.
8. Close the top lid and cook for 10 minutes. Now open the top lid, flip the pieces and top with the cheese.
9. Close the top lid and cook for 5 more minutes. Serve warm with the chives and ranch dressing on top.

Nutritional Values (Per Serving):
Calories: 534
Fat: 34g
Saturated Fat: 13g
Trans Fat: 0g
Carbohydrates: 14.5g
Fiber: 4g
Sodium: 1359mg
Protein: 31g

Made in the USA
Monee, IL
18 December 2019